CREATING A SCENE IN CORINTH
A SIMULATION

"Among thousands of publications on Paul's letters, *Creating a Scene* stands out as a unique and creative approach. It invites readers to enter into conversation with the apostle and his conflicted Christian community."
—*David Pettegrew, Corinthian historian and archaeologist, editor of the blog* Corinthian Matters

"This book is good Bible study with 'play.' It will advance Bible literacy as participants gain entry into the mission and work of the apostle Paul and learn basics of Christian belief and moral praxis."
—*Willard Swartley, professor emeritus at Anabaptist Mennonite Biblical Seminary, author of the Believers Church Bible Commentary* John

CREATING A SCENE IN CORINTH

A SIMULATION

RETA HALTEMAN FINGER AND GEORGE D. MCCLAIN

 **Herald Press**

Harrisonburg, Virginia
Waterloo, Ontario

Library of Congress Catalog-in-Publication Data
Creating a scene in Corinth : a simulation / by Reta Halteman
Finger and George D. McClain.
    pages cm
    Includes bibliographical references and index.
    ISBN 978-0-8361-9711-2 (pbk. : alk. paper) 1. Bible. Corinthians,
1st—Criticism, interpretation, etc. 2.   Bible. Corinthians, 1st—
Study and teaching—Simulation methods. I. Title.
    BS2675.52.F55 2013
    227'.206—dc23
                                                        2013002207

NOTE ON THE BIBLE READINGS:
The extended 1 Corinthians texts included in chapters 8 through
16, intended for presentation in simulation settings, are the authors'
own translations of the text of Paul's letter, and may be abridged.
The renderings are drawn from the New Revised Standard Version
and a range of other translations, as well as the *Greek New
Testament*.

For all other quotations, unless otherwise noted, Scripture text is
quoted, with permission, from the *New Revised Standard Version*,
© 1989, Division of Christian Education of the National Council of
Churches of Christ in the United States of America.

CREATING A SCENE IN CORINTH
Copyright © 2013 by Herald Press, Harrisonburg, Virginia 22802
    Released simultaneously in Canada by Herald Press,
    Waterloo, Ontario N2L 6H7. All rights reserved.
Library of Congress Control Number: 2013002207
International Standard Book Number: 978-0-8361-9711-2
Printed in United States of America
Cover design by Paul Stocksdale

17 16 15 14 13   10 9 8 7 6 5 4 3 2 1

To order or request information, please call 1-800-245-7894 in the
U.S. or 1-800-631-6535 in Canada. Or visit www.heraldpress.com.

*To all those who energized this book
by re-creating Chloe's house church.*

TABLE OF CONTENTS

7

Part II—The Play Begins! Reenacting Chloe's House Church

SUPPLEMENTARY WEB RESOURCES

For additional resources to complement this book, please visit www.HeraldPress.com/CreatingAScene. These include:

1. A Visit to Ancient Corinth (slide presentation)
2. Time Travel to Ancient Corinth (slide presentation)
3. Publicity Announcement for Adult Sunday School Simulation of 1 Corinthians
4. Representative Speeches from Chloe's House Church
5. Worshiping with the Corinthians
6. A Visitor's Guide to Corinth
7. Extra Material for Character Development in Corinth
8. Using *Creating a Scene in Corinth: A Simulation* in College or Seminary

FOREWORD

This book is an invitation to a communal voyage of discovery. In contrast to the often abstract and single-themed approaches that characterize many studies of 1 Corinthians, the simulations created by Reta Finger and George McClain reveal the wide range of intellectual and emotional meanings of Paul's letter for a highly diverse audience both then and now. However, while this mode of study is serious and requires a lot of work, let there be no mistake: this process is also a lot of fun.

The simulation approach is related to a major new development in biblical scholarship to which I have been privileged to be a contributor. In a 1983 collaboration with pioneering scholars such as David Rhoads, Joanna Dewey, and Werner Kelber, I initiated a new research group in the Society of Biblical Literature named The Bible in Ancient and Modern Media. The purpose of this group was to research the formation and distribution of the biblical tradition in the communication cultures of the ancient world and in the far more complex mix of the communication cultures of the modern world.

While form criticism had established the origins of the traditions of the Bible in oral culture, the operative assumption of many modern readers has been that once the traditions were written down they were part of a fully literate culture. As a result, the Bible has been studied as a series of texts that were read by readers—usually individually and in silence. Even when there has been a recognition that the letters of Paul, for example, were read aloud to the various Pauline churches, the methodology of biblical scholars has been to study the texts in silence.

The recent investigation of the media culture of antiquity has made it clear that this picture and methodology are inadequate. Rates of literacy in the ancient world were low: 5 to 15 per cent. Manuscripts were copied by hand and were relatively expensive. While there was a lively trade in manuscripts, only rich people and communities collected them. Local communities had manuscripts of individual books of the Bible, but few had the complete text that we now have in our printed Bibles. The primary means for the publication of books was by performance for audiences— sometimes from a manuscript but often from memory.

If we want to explore the meaning of the Bible in its original context, therefore, we need to perform the Bible for audiences and listen for its meaning and impact among ancient audiences. Furthermore, the methods of biblical scholarship need to be based on hearing and performing biblical compositions rather than reading the texts in silence. This new methodology is now being called "performance criticism."

The interpretation of the Bible as performance literature is increasingly being perceived as a new paradigm for biblical scholarship. This approach sheds new light on the meaning of the various biblical compositions in their original context. It is also more congruent with the post-literate culture of the digital age with its preference for multimedia rather than text-only productions. When performed well for audiences now, compositions such as 1 Corinthians have a new vitality in contrast to the tepid character of traditional reading. *Creating a Scene in Corinth* can appropriately be named as a performance criticism project. Its focus on the performance of Paul's composition as heard by representative Corinthian believers will enable contemporary communities to experience the theological power and deep emotional impact of Paul's appeal to his beloved community. The book is grounded in the collective wisdom that has emerged from archeological, sociological and textual research on first-century Corinth in all its glory and squalor.

This project is the culmination of a lifetime of study and experience by two gifted scholars and teachers. Its publication is particularly joyful for me because George and I lived across the hall from each other at Union Theological Seminary in the early '60's and have been friends ever since. Their book is part of a wider movement within the community of biblical scholarship that seeks to bring new vitality and precision to the interpretation of the Bible, both in its original context and in the global community today.

> —*Thomas E. Boomershine*
> *Professor of New Testament*
> *Emeritus*
> *Founder of the Network of*
> *Biblical Storytellers*

INTRODUCTION

"Yes!" insist the members of the Apollos faction to each other. "We like our house church the way it is. Why should it matter if we eat our suppers before you all get here?"

"After all," adds Patron Valerius, "We deserve our privileges. We're the job creators!"

"Oh really?" protest some of the slaves, exercising their newly acquired "in-Christ" self-images. "You've given us all the jobs—but without pay! And by the time we're finished working and can come to supper, the food is all gone—and you're already drunk!"

It's a one-hour Sunday school class in the church I (Reta) grew up in. I'm the guest teacher, and we're reenacting a church fight that happened back in the first century.

After a background sketch, the class has divided into the four quarreling factions named in 1 Corinthians 1:12. Now the wealthy, educated patrons and fans of Apollos are defending themselves against lower-class factions of those supporting Paul, the law-observant Jews backing Peter, and women slaves who insist "Christ alone" is their mentor and savior.

Paul's harsh critique of their regular *agape* meals is read (1 Corinthians 11:17-34). Paul declares that their meal is *not* a Supper of the Lord, and it would be better if they didn't have it at all.

Then the class dives in, as depicted above. And when the dust settles, they begin making connections to social and economic inequalities in our communities today. The conversation spills over into the session the following week. Whoever would have thought Bible study could be so much *fun?*

Simulation: it's been done before—let's do it again!

My first attempt at reenacting biblical house churches was with Paul's letter to the Roman Christians. Research by various Pauline scholars and the list of names in Romans 16 enabled me to create a simulation that has been used in Sunday schools and church groups, in college and seminary classes, as well as for personal study.[1] Since then I've wanted to do the same for 1 Corinthians because the issues in that letter are so compelling and relevant.

In a similar way I (George) have found reenactment and role-play to be powerful tools. When I was being trained for participation in the 1964 Mississippi Freedom Summer voter registration project, we acted out being assaulted by toughs who pushed and shoved and called us racial epithets. In a workshop with New Testament scholar Walter Wink, I was the woman with late-arriving guests pounding on a neighbor's door at midnight asking for bread—Jesus' parable about the urgency of prayer (Luke 11:5-8). I am deeply grateful for such experiences that have illuminated my life. Having used Reta's Romans reenactment and my own Corinthian role-play in teaching, I am delighted to join forces for this project.

WHAT WE LEARN AND HOW WE LEARN

In a way, this book has a double emphasis—in terms of both content (what we learn) and method (how we learn). In our churches most of us are exposed to what is called the "doctrinal" model of biblical interpretation. That perspective sees the Bible as containing timeless truths clearly set forth for people in any age and culture. Much is to be gained from this, but when we limit ourselves to this model, we miss out on the insights acquired from knowing the historical and social situation out of which a text

---

1. Finger, *Paul and the Roman House Churches: A Simulation.*

This Roman road leads from the center of Corinth north toward the Port of Lechaion.

was written. And sometimes we get it wrong by confusing timeless truths with cultural practices from another age.

Over the past fifty years or so, many advances have been made in understanding the cultural context of biblical texts. And since the 1990s, much biblical, historical, and archaeological scholarship has been converging into what is called an "empire-critical" approach.[2] The Jesus Movement was born under the powerful and often ruthless thumb of the Roman Empire. In so many ways, the values and practices of Jesus' gospel directly confronted the Roman "domination system,"[3] a hierarchy where wealth and power were concentrated at the top and hard work and poverty at the bottom. Small house churches with converts only a year or two removed from such "empire" ways of thinking and acting spurred missionaries like Paul to keep on proclaiming a radically different message. We think lay Christians deserve to know these insights—especially because we are consciously and unconsciously so influenced by "empire" values today.

---

2. "Critical" in the sense of *analyzing*.

3. "Domination system" is a term popularized by Walter Wink, to describe interlocking structures of control and oppression.

We also focus on *how* we learn. We wrote this book in the form of a reenactment, a sort of drama you can role-play. Your task is to live into the very early Christian community to which Paul was writing. Each of you assumes the character of one member: Jew or Gentile, wealthy or poor, woman or man, freeborn, freed, or enslaved, conservative or liberal. Each character has an occupation and a particular role in the house church. You might be Erastus in the city treasurer's office, or Deborah, a slave midwife. Chapters 3 through 7 provide general background about first-century Corinth to help each of you develop your character.

You may be familiar with the Mennonite actor Ted Swartz, who has been performing for twenty-five years on the knife-edge between the sacred and the profane, the profound and the hilarious. Swartz identifies three prerequisites for good acting: (1) be present in the moment, (2) listen to the other actors on stage, and (3) use empathy to put yourself into the shoes, clothes, and pain of another person. He compares good acting to living a faithful life: "The very act of crawling inside a character is the same act as embracing the other, seeing through the eyes of the other, loving your enemy."[4] Our impromptu reenactments will rarely attain standards of stage acting, but the same principles are at work.

Identifying with another person in a different time and culture uses your right and left brains and helps you retain what you have learned. In addition, educational research shows that people learn more effectively through debate, constructive controversy and experiential learning than through either lecture or group discussion.[5]

HOW DOES THE ROLE-PLAY WORK?

Would you like to join in? You will learn much content by simply reading this book by yourself, but you will gain more experientially if a group simulates Chloe's house church. We focus primarily on laypeople in churches who

---

4. Bishop, "Gathering Explores Anabaptist Message in Visual Age," 12.
5. Johnson, Johnson, and Smith, "Constructive Controversy: The Educative Power of Intellectual Conflict," 29–37.

enjoy interacting in groups, such as Sunday school or home study groups—though no one will fall asleep if the simulation is used in college and seminary courses either! Simulation can also happen in other settings, such as a weekend conference or camp.

When the group is ready for simulation, the leader (or whoever plays Stephanas or Phoebe) reads aloud a portion of the letter to Chloe's house church. Each participant listens carefully to what Paul says in the letter and decides how to react to it—*in character*. (Do not follow along in your Bible; most of you in the first century cannot read!) At the time Paul wrote, he did not know he was writing what we today know as Scripture. Many first-century Christians must have disagreed with Paul in major or minor ways—and were quite free to speak their minds! Role-play encourages disagreement, which sharpens our thinking and helps us enter into the experience of the earliest Christians.

After the simulation there is a time for debriefing and application. The time machine turns off, and we are our twenty-first century selves again. We evaluate what happened in the simulation. Did we stay in character? How did the experience help us understand what Paul meant? How do Paul's strong convictions make sense for our lives today? Each chapter will contain questions to stimulate discussion, both as part of the simulation and then for today's application.[6]

WHO SHOULD LEAD THE SIMULATION?

The best leader is not necessarily a "teacher"—in the sense of someone who knows a lot of information and can lecture well. Instead, the group will need an enthusiastic organizer, someone who can set the stage for learning and guide group discussions. The leader must be prepared for learning that is not always systematic but is highly participatory. A sense of humor helps; those most in touch with

---

6. Throughout the simulation, we may refer to background material about which different scholars do not necessarily agree. Such issues can provide opportunity for discussion and debate within the simulation or in the application period afterward.

their own humanity can best bring out the humanity of Paul and his Corinthian audience. An attitude of creativity, innovation, and risk-taking will be an asset. A participant in one of our reenactments put it this way: "As a former teacher, I applaud your efforts to bring about new ways for people to learn such material so they can integrate it into their lives. When people use this method, they use their highest level of thinking skills."

An introductory background simulation and the Leader's Guide are included as appendix 1 and appendix 2, respectively, at the back of this book. Other supplementary instructions and resources can be found at the book's web page at www.HeraldPress.com/CreatingAScene:

1. A Visit to Ancient Corinth (slide presentation)
2. Time Travel to Ancient Corinth (slide presentation)
3. Publicity Announcement
   To attract participants to your coming simulation study, this short skit can be used in a public meeting or worship service.
4. Representative speeches from Chloe's house church
   These character sketches are useful if you have only one or two sessions.
5. Worshiping with the Corinthians
   Ideas and plans for six concurrent worship services on 1 Corinthians.
6. A Visitor's Guide to Corinth
   A brief introduction for visitors who drop in on Chloe's house church simulation.
7. Extra Material for Character Development
   If you have more than nineteen participants, use this information to create more characters.
8. Using *Creating a Scene in Corinth: A Simulation* in College or Seminary

Blessings to you as you explore the "scene" at one unruly house church in Corinth, in a busy, materialistic culture that often resembles our own.

PART I

SETTING THE STAGE,
GATHERING THE PROPS

1

FROM EPHESUS TO CORINTH— BEARING AN EXPLOSIVE LETTER

◫◫◫◫◫◫◫◫◫◫◫◫◫◫

Early June, 54 CE, on the Aegean Sea between Asia Minor (Turkey) and Achaia (Greece). Four travelers— three men and a woman—squinted into the western sun as they stood on the deck of a small ship sailing on the Aegean Sea toward their destination, Corinth's seaport in southern Greece. Ahead of them, the afternoon sun back-lit the Isthmus ridge hiding the mighty Acrocorinth, the mountain protecting the city below and crowned with the temple of Aphrodite, goddess of erotic passion.

Stephanas (1 Corinthians 16:17) squeezed his wife Julia's hand as they neared the port town of Cenchreae on the Isthmus of Corinth. He was both excited and appre-hensive. Rolled up inside his tunic lay a precious letter from their brother in Christ, Paul of Tarsus—longer and more detailed than any Paul had ever written before. Its contents were potentially explosive and he and Julia were charged with reading it to people who may not want to hear it. At least they had the support of their comrades, Fortunatus and Achaicus.

For Fortunatus and Achaicus (1 Corinthians 16:17), this calm sea of early summer was a welcome contrast to their April trip in the opposite direction across the Aegean to Ephesus.

Two months earlier . . . Because of unpredictable weather, most shipping took place only between late May and November. But Chloe, their employer and a house church leader in Corinth (1 Corinthians 1:11), had not wanted to wait. She had been worried sick about the quarreling and tensions pervading most of the house churches in the region. To add to the distress, scanty rainfall over the winter portended another serious drought and a poor summer harvest. This would increase the general unrest and widen the gap between the haves and the have-nots.

Surely Paul would know what to do—but he was planting churches in Ephesus. Chloe had appealed to Phoebe, another house church leader (Romans 16:1-2), and the owner of a shipping firm in Corinth's eastern port of Cenchreae. Phoebe was willing to send one of her smaller ships to Ephesus with an early cargo, so Chloe had dispatched two of her employees, Fortunatus and Achaicus, to report to Paul on the growing crisis. Despite the risk at sea, the young men were eager to travel. Never having left the Corinthia, they had only heard of Ephesus's magnificent library, colossal theater, and sidewalks of inlaid mosaics.

Meanwhile, on the other side of Corinth . . . While Chloe and her household were making these arrangements, Stephanas and Julia were equally alarmed at what was happening to the house churches on their side of the city. As Christian leaders, they had consulted with other church members in Corinth—mostly those with some education or aspirations to public office—both Gentiles and Jews.

The result was a letter that they had personally taken to Paul in mid-May. It contained a list of questions and comments about how they should conduct their lives as worshipers of Jesus rather than of the emperor in Rome. Believers from different classes and backgrounds in their assemblies had differing ideas—hence, the friction. Some were annoyed by Paul's comments in an earlier letter about not associating with their "immoral" pagan friends and neighbors (see 1 Corinthians 5:9).

Arriving in Ephesus, Stephanas and Julia had found Paul in the tent-making shop off Kouretes Street that he rented with Prisca (Priscilla) and Aquila. They also met Sosthenes, the former synagogue official in Corinth who had taken the rap for Paul the day angry Jews hauled him before the governor (Acts 18:12-17). Sosthenes had lost his leadership position at the synagogue, because his sympathies for the Jesus movement became known. He eventually joined Paul in Ephesus, reaching out to the Jewish community there.

Each evening after the shop closed at sunset, the believers shared a simple meal—a supper of the Lord, as Paul named it—with any converted or interested Ephesians who came. Then followed several hours of discussion or even heated debate about the nature of Paul's gospel and what he needed to tell his struggling assemblies in Corinth.

Writing the letter

Before the arrival of Stephanas and Julia, Paul and Sosthenes had already begun a letter of response to the Corinthian Christians. Fortunatus and Achaicus had told them all about the troubles. The carefully worded theology of the first section had given way to shock and outrage at some of the stories the men recounted. (Andronicus did what?!) Now Paul also had to respond to this letter the Corinthian believers had sent to him. Through these weeks of prayer and conversation, the Spirit had gradually given them wisdom and insight.

Paul did not have a scribal hand, so he dictated his letter to Prisca, a well-educated daughter of a Roman noble. Stephanas often went to sleep in the flickering light of an oil lamp, listening to the low tones of dictation and the

Ancient harbor at Cenchreae, Corinth's port on the Saronic Gulf and Aegean Sea. Paul's coworker Phoebe heads a house church in this town. Paul's letter arrives here by ship from Ephesus across the Aegean Sea in Asia Minor.

scratch of pen on papyrus. Paul signed the letter with his own hand, affirming his love and concern for all his flock in Corinth.

HOME TO CORINTH

Now this very scroll burned inside Stephanas's tunic. As the harbor at Cenchreae grew larger in the distance, he could see the docks and the small temple of the goddess Isis just behind them. Finally the captain maneuvered the ship past the fishnets and docked the boat.

The four travelers disembarked and walked along the shore to the house of Phoebe, leader of the Jesus-believers who lived in this port city. They would spend the night with her family and in the morning depart for Corinth, ten kilometers to the west.

Though eager for home, the travelers shared their worries with each other as they approached Phoebe's house. How would the believers take Paul's letter? They were not comfortable with everything in it themselves. Gifted in rhetoric, Paul had not minced words. Now this letter must be read to each assembly of believers as forcefully as possible. At least Phoebe, like Prisca, trusted Paul and knew how to handle his passions and anxieties. Hopefully she would help interpret the letter to those whom Paul was most strongly criticizing.

In the meantime, the travelers received a joyful welcome from Phoebe's household as they embraced each other in the growing twilight.

June 2009 CE, the Corinthia, Greece

The characters in the scene just described were long gone when we (Reta and George) were part of a small group spending ten days in Greece, exploring the ruins of ancient Corinth and the surrounding region called the Corinthia. We spent two days with Dr. David Pettegrew, a professor of Roman history at Messiah College and an archeologist who spends summers digging in Cyprus and Corinth. Besides the ancient city center where tourists visit, David led us through weeds and rocks to other ancient remains we would never have found on our own.

Of special interest was a freestanding private villa with space enough to handle a small assembly of twenty to twenty-five people. Is this the sort of house where Stephanas and Julia lived—or could they only afford renting a tenement apartment?

A spiritual highlight awaited at the remains of Corinth's eastern port, Cenchreae. We sat on the rocks of an ancient stone dock, kicking our feet in the peaceful waters of the Aegean. We imagined Paul saying goodbye to his Corinthian brothers and sisters, then sailing from this spot with his coworkers, Prisca and Aquila, to plant churches in Ephesus (Acts 18:18-21). Where was Phoebe's house? Did she really own a shipping company which would have given her enough wealth to serve as patron to Paul and other Christian leaders? The Spirit hovered here, as real as sea gulls flapping overhead.

The papyrus scroll that Stephanas carried to Corinth (as we imagine it) has long ago disintegrated. But its words lived on, painstakingly copied over and over and read aloud in churches throughout the Roman Empire. Finally the letter was bound into a collection and viewed as authoritative for the Christian church as a whole.

Translated from Greek into Latin and uncounted other
languages, today it is part of our Bible, one of the thirteen
letters attributed to the apostle Paul.

A LOVE-HATE RELATIONSHIP WITH PAUL

How you hear Paul's words depends a lot on which church
tradition you come from. In some, you hear more sermons
from Paul's letters than any other part of the Bible. Paul's
words are seen as literally God's words, applied directly
to you or your congregation. Many Pauline texts sustain
your spiritual life—though perhaps others induce guilt or
inadequacy.

On the other hand, you may not like Paul. You think
he's a hoary old conservative, out of touch with the
twenty-first century. He's bossy, domineering, pro-slavery,
anti-women, and anti-gay, you think. Leave Paul alone
and stick with Jesus and the four Gospels!

Or maybe you're somewhere in between. Like the first
group, you are spiritually sustained when Paul writes about
faith, hope, and love. With Paul you work for unity and
desire to be "in Christ." But you ignore or wince at what he
writes in other places. Paul arouses mixed emotions.

But is there yet another way to look at Paul? Can we put
ourselves in the place of those first-century believers who
knew Paul *before* his letters were considered Scripture,
when they felt free to argue and debate with him? Can we
see him as one charismatic evangelist among others?

The intent of this book is to interact with Paul's Corinthian
letter as if we really were those Christians in Corinth. Then,
as we more clearly experience what Paul *meant* in the first
century, we can better understand what his writings *mean* in
our twenty-first century context. Indeed, if we do not do so,
we will often get it wrong, sometimes with hurtful results.

BRIDGING THE TIME AND CULTURE GAP

It is not easy to recreate the context of a letter nearly 2000
years old. We must remember the apt phrase, "The past is
a foreign country. They do things differently there."[1] We

---

1. Lowenthal, *The Past Is a Foreign Country*, xvi; derived from L. P.
Hartley's novel, *The Go-Between*, 1953.

must explain the unquestioned use of slaves, the practice of killing animals to appease the gods, the odd sexual behaviors of converted pagans, the reasons why veils were worn or not worn, or the high esteem in which ecstatic speech was held.

Rome's inhabitants would have ridiculed Western concepts of democracy and the "self-evident" Enlightenment ideal that "all people are created equal." Nothing was more "self-evident" to them than that people were *not* created equal.

But for all that, human nature has changed very little. We face many of the same issues in our society and religious institutions that Paul confronted: competition, polarization, greed, one-upmanship, sex addictions and infidelities, issues of food and hunger, gender and ethnic inequalities, diverse religious practices, fear of illness and death, tensions between worship of God and allegiance to one's country.

Our reflection on 1 Corinthians and our research into its cultural background have led us to the conclusion that the basic issue for Paul in this letter is one of social class, status, and the insidious impact of the corrupt values of the Roman Empire. Hierarchies were everywhere. Patrons and clients were bound to each other by tight relationships of inequality. Women were considered by nature to be inferior to men. Wealth was created on the backs of enslaved bodies with no rights whatsoever. Everyone was locked into "their place" in a tight pyramid. At the top sat the emperor, high priest of an imperial religion which justified this hierarchy as normal, necessary, and ordained by the gods.

Against this immovable object of imperial religion and domination, Paul hurled the irresistible force of Jesus' gospel of radical equality, shared community, and salvation open to all. How did he do it—and did he succeed?

In chapter 2, a readers theater contrasts powerful pagan aristocrats in Corinth with the more humble Jesus-assemblies Paul addressed in his letter. You will join some "time travelers" in a tour of the main square of Roman Corinth, led by an actual Corinthian aristocrat of the time, Babbius Italicus. Watch him bask in the glow of his famous father, Babbius Philinus.

You are also invited to act out—in costume, if you can—a scene found in appendix 1, "Arrogant Aristocrats in Action." At a grand reception before the opening of the Isthmian Games, the Corinthian elite display the haughtiness, arrogance, and devotion to imperial religion for which they were so well known. Welcome to Corinth!

2

WELCOME, TIME TRAVELERS!

A GUIDED TOUR OF CORINTH

🏛🏛🏛🏛🏛🏛🏛🏛🏛

Understanding the past is always a mind exercise in time travel. To introduce you to Corinth in Roman times, we have created a hypothetical but historically plausible dialogue between an influential Corinthian (who actually did live at the time) and three time travelers from the twenty-first century who ask questions we ourselves might ask. We imagine this dialogue occurring at the time of the arrival of Paul's first letter to the Corinthians, that is, 54 CE.[1]

Babbius Italicus: Hail, visitors! *Ave*! We are thrilled to have you here in Corinth, "the Aphrodite of cities." The colonial travel office wants me to give you a tour of our city's glorious Forum and to answer your questions. I am Babbius Italicus, a prominent citizen of new Corinth. It's my factory that makes the best of the famous Corinthian bronzes. And I have a very personal connection to this great Forum, which I'll explain shortly.

Skeptical Time Traveler: First off, Mr. Babbius, why is it so smoky around here?

---

1. Go to www.HeraldPress.com/CreatingAScene for accompanying color photos which can be projected in a session where this chapter is acted out.

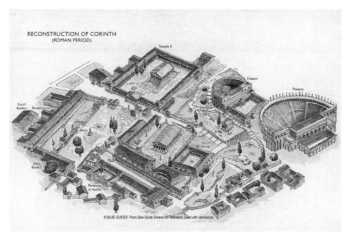

This reconstruction of the center city of first-century Roman Corinth includes the Forum, offices, temples, shops, baths, and a theater.

> **Babbius Italicus:** What do you mean? There's smoke in any city. You must know that! The smoke comes from people cooking their food and burning trash.

> **Skeptical Time Traveler:** But what's that weird smell? Ugh!

> **Babbius Italicus:** That special smell is from the roasting flesh of animal sacrifices. See the priests at the

central altar sacrificing to the gods and the imperial family? It's the smoke that carries the sacrifice up to the gods. Surely you make sacrifices where you come from, don't you?

Skeptical Time Traveler: It looks awfully bloody!

Babbius Italicus: That's because the priest has just cut the throat of that magnificent bull and placed it on the sacred fire as an offering to Athena, goddess of war. The priests are pleading with Athena to protect our great city, especially now with the return of the famine. . . .

Let me give you a bit of orientation. We're standing at the great new archway where the Lechaion Road enters the Forum. Now rising off to your right is the magnificent, ancient temple to Apollo, Son of Zeus. You know, in the civil war it was Apollo who gave Caesar Augustus his great victory over Marc Antony, finally bringing peace. The divine Augustus, son of god, was deeply devoted to Apollo and led a revival of the people's religious devotion all across the empire.

Archway from road into Forum

Inquisitive Time Traveler: Didn't you say "the divine Augustus"? Do you mean that you Corinthians actually worship your rulers as gods?

Babbius Italicus: As we're talking let's walk to the west here along this wonderful colonnade. To answer your question—well, it's more complicated than that. People in the eastern part of our empire like to think of the emperor as a god. We here give him great honor because he is the representative of the gods on earth, and we wish to receive their favor. They have the power of life and death over us. Caesars Julius and Augustus, for example, were hailed as divine when omens confirmed it at their deaths. You see, we are a very devout and religious people.

Inquisitive Time Traveler: Who decides that the emperors are divine?

Babbius Italicus: Officially, the Senate in Rome decides. They have declared Augustus, Tiberius, and now Claudius to be sons of god and have raised the whole imperial family to divine status.

To celebrate this endless line of splendor, we built the new temple to the west, right above the string of shops. It sits higher than any other temple. It's dedicated to Octavia, the sister of Caesar Augustus, and honors the divinity and majesty of the entire imperial line. If you go inside you'll see a magnificent statue of Augustus with all the trappings of the goddess Athena.

Caesar Augustus

Skeptical Time Traveler: That sounds really crazy.

Babbius Italicus: You may think so, but let me tell you something. Our whole life as a society is ordered around our devotion to the gods and to the imperial family. With all our people's differences, it's what holds us together: Greek or Roman, barbarian or civilized, slave or free, rich or poor, male or female.

Octavia Temple

Skeptical Time Traveler: I still don't understand; it sounds weird to me.

Babbius Italicus: Well, think what you will. But don't you dare act out your irreverence and atheism while you're here. You will endanger Corinth's welfare, and if you do, we simply cannot guarantee your safety. So I advise you to touch your lips in respect when you pass a temple or an altar.

Skeptical Time Traveler: Okay, "When in Rome do as the Romans do."

Babbius Italicus: Right now feelings of piety and patriotism are running especially high: the emperor has just designated Corinth the sponsor for new province-wide observances of imperial worship. All the cities of Achaia, southern Greece, that is, will be contributing to this. For instance, the entire province will celebrate Caesar Augustus's birthday of September 23, not just in September, but on the twenty-third of every month!

Skeptical Time Traveler: But what about the separation between church and state? Between religion and politics?

Babbius Italicus: I don't know what you mean by "church" or "state," but let me just say that here religion is politics, and politics is religion. It's just common sense. For instance, the current famine, which is stirring up the common people, shows that we've offended the gods, and it's a political problem and a religious issue at the same time.

Inquisitive Time Traveler: Is that why your coins usually show both the emperor or magistrate and a god?

Babbius Italicus: Don't your coins back home? One of your time travelers once said that your own coins have both the image of a famous ruler and the words "In God We Trust." That makes total sense to us. You also have "E Pluribus Unum"[2] on your coins—and in our Latin language, of all things. Later you can

---

2. "Out of many, one."

Roman coins and American penny

explain that to me. Here's my showroom: Babbius Bronzes.

Enthusiastic Time Traveler: Tell us more about Corinthian bronzes!

Examples of Corinthian bronzes

Babbius Italicus: We use a secret alloy of bronze, sometimes containing gold or silver, to create beautiful items for religious use, such as statues of gods and heroes, incense holders, and bowls for offerings, also gorgeous items for banquet or decorative use. Corinth has produced these prized pieces of art for several centuries and they have become collectors' items. In fact, Emperor Tiberius was such an avid collector of Corinthian bronzes that he had a certain steward do nothing else but care for his magnificent collection. Take a quick look at my showroom and then let's move along.

Enthusiastic Time Traveler: Mr. Babbius, what's that cool circle of columns up ahead?

Babbius Italicus: So glad you asked. If I may boast for a moment, I must say I am so proud that right alongside this row of temples is this monument that my very own father Babbius Philinus erected. He wanted to show his piety and to celebrate his many outstanding contributions to Corinth. I'm so proud of how far my father—a former slave, mind you—was able to rise. O, blest be his memory.

Monument of Babbius Philinus

Enthusiastic Time Traveler: Wow! Your father actually was born a slave and became so famous?

Babbius Italicus: Yes, he was born a slave in Rome. Luckily a slave trader sold my father to a kind master here in Corinth, where, being a new city, all things were possible. His name shows he was a slave—*Philinus* means "dear one." That's not the elegant name an aristocrat would be given at birth—like the name Italicus he gave me to honor Rome. With hard work, a brilliant mind, and the favor of the gods he eventually bought his own freedom. He made a fortune, held many public offices, served as priest in the imperial cult, and became one of the leading citizens in Corinth since its refounding almost one hundred years ago.

Now, let's walk east across the middle of the Forum. That will give us a closer look at the central altar. I know it's rather crowded today. It's a market day and lots of people from the city and countryside are here, as well as the usual merchants, tourists, workers, and slaves.

Skeptical Time Traveler: What did you mean, "refounding?" And "Roman" Corinth? I thought Corinth was an ancient Greek city.

Babbius Italicus: My fellow nobles don't like us to talk about it, but since you asked, let me say that there are really two Corinths, one ancient and Greek, the other modern and Roman. Ancient Corinth was a prosperous city that represented much of what is the best of Greek civilization.

 Only two hundred years ago, when the gods were passing on the mantle of destiny and empire to Rome, Corinth led the horribly misguided Greek military resistance against Rome's benevolence. The gods had willed that the Romans were ordained to spread protection, peace and security across the peoples of the Mediterranean Sea. Corinth was an obstacle to that sacred mission and had to be eliminated.

Skeptical Time Traveler: You mean to say the gods deliberately willed the destruction of old Corinth?

Babbius Italicus: Well, yes. General Mummius was called upon to fulfill the divine plan by destroying Corinth as a city. For a hundred years it lay in ruins. Men were killed; women and children enslaved. They paid the price for resisting Rome's divine destiny. Not much was left—only a few Greeks returned, making crafts and doing some trading. But then about a hundred years ago Julius Caesar saw the potential for a new city, a Roman city, and refounded Corinth as a beacon of *Romanitas.*

Inquisitive Time Traveler: What's Ro-man-i-tas?

Babbius Italicus: That's our Latin word for civilization, the best ever. After the refounding, eager colonists came from Rome and all over to ensure that Corinth reflected all the glory that is Rome. All the genius of Rome was brought to the rebuilding of Corinth. We laid out the streets in the Roman grid pattern, and built this impressive new Roman Forum. Our ports have been enlarged, our roads and plazas paved. Numerous temples have been built and restored. We have a grand theater, marvelous baths, and an enviable water system.

Skeptical Time Traveler: If Romanitas is so great, then why do we read back home that most of your people are dirt poor, almost half are slaves, very many women die in childbirth, and people can only expect to live thirty years?

Babbius Italicus: Look, for most people, hasn't this always been the case, and won't it always be so? It's always a matter of the cream rising to the top. A certain small group is born to rule, to advance the arts and cultivate wisdom, to offer the sacrifices. The gods then appoint the larger masses of men to follow those who lead, to do the day-to-day work, to build the roads, repair the temples, build the baths and theaters, grow the olives and grain, to fight the wars. And for the women to raise the children and cook the food. That's what women are for. Everyone has a place, and for some that means being slaves. The common good is served when everyone knows their place and lives out their destiny with piety, obedience, and diligence.

Enthusiastic Time Traveler: We've all been taught that the Roman Empire was the greatest of all ancient societies, and it's great to see it up close. What's that *awesome* mountain in front of us?

Babbius Italicus: That famous mountain is the natural landmark of our city; it is called Acrocorinth, or Upper Corinth. According to some, the ancient historic temple to Aphrodite up on top once had a

thousand priestesses to offer hospitality. Halfway up the mountain is the sanctuary of Demeter, goddess of earth, harvest, forests, and agriculture, and Kore, her daughter, queen of the underworld. The Forum, you see, is set between these two ancient landmarks, the Acrocorinth and, behind you, the Temple of Apollo.

Inquisitive Time Traveler: What's that platform right in the middle of the Forum, behind the central altar and the statue of Athena?

Babbius Italicus: Glad you asked. That is the *bema* or rostrum, where our magistrates address the people, conduct elections, or mete out their wise judgments in cases of dispute—the famous blind justice of Rome. Each year on election day you would see this entire lower Forum crowded with the male citizens to choose our two mayors, our *duovirs*, for their one-year terms.

Inquisitive Time Traveler: In our sacred Scriptures back home, there's an account about one of your leaders, a Gallio, who ruled on a case involving a Paul of Tarsus. He had been accused of leading other Jews astray. Do you know anything about that?

Bema, "place of judgment"

Babbius Italicus: I myself don't remember anything about that. There are lots of internal quarrels within the various sects and associations here in Corinth. Those Jews really create problems all out of proportion to their small numbers, like wanting to be exempt from our religious and patriotic observances and insisting on getting meat butchered in weird ways. They are atheists, you know, with no respect at all for the gods—but because they have ancient traditions and we Romans respect ancient traditions, we allow them to practice their strange ways. But they can cause trouble and, as you may know, the divine Emperor Claudius had to expel them from Rome several years ago. So we do keep a very close eye on them. And you're right, whenever Proconsul Gallio issued a ruling, this is exactly where he would do it.

Enthusiastic Time Traveler: Behind the *bema* is that enormously long building with columns. What's that beautiful colonnade for?

Babbius Italicus: It is impressive, isn't it? We sometimes call it the South Stoa, the South Porches. Beautifully done, it serves many purposes. It's a

South Porches

shopping mall, as well as the nerve center of provincial and local government. In the center is the *Bouleuterion*, or city council chamber, with benches all around the large room; and over on the left end are several offices related to the Panhellenic Games sponsored by Corinth.

These rooms are magnificently decorated with gorgeous mosaics showing athletes in action, and the president of the games has his office there.

Inquisitive Time Traveler: Are you talking about the Olympic Games?

Babbius Italicus: Not exactly. Our famous games are one of the four Greek-wide games; there are games at Olympia, Nemea, and Delphi. We think ours, the Isthmian Games—named after the Isthmus of Corinth—are the best. Being president of the games is the highest honor one could have here in Corinth. Let's continue on toward the Julian Basilica.

(Shouting) How dare you stumble in front of me,

slave girl! Watch out whom you're messing with! Take this slap in the face; this will teach you to stay out of my way! Get up and get out of here before I go to your master! And quit crying! Get going!

(Disgustedly) Slaves these days are so careless and stupid—except the really good ones like my managers. This girl doesn't

Well-preserved stadium at Epidaurus south of Corinth

look like she's worth the trouble to feed and clothe. On second thought, maybe she's worth it in bed. She *is* a real pretty one . . .

Skeptical Time Traveler: Excuse me?

Babbius Italicus: That's exactly what young slaves are best for. We owners sometimes swap slaves so we don't get bored in bed—girl slaves and boy slaves, too. And if the girls get pregnant, then we get another slave for free.

Skeptical Time Traveler: That's disgusting.

Babbius Italicus: You certainly don't seem to understand how things work around here. A slave owner owns his slave's body and his slave's children. It's always been that way and always will be. We're now in front of the Julian Basilica, erected in honor of all the imperial descendants of Julius Caesar. I'd love to take you in there to see all the magnificent statues of gods and the imperial family—many of them made in my factory—but I see the law court is still in session.

Inquisitive Time Traveler: What's that big inscription in front of the basilica?

Babbius Italicus: That's about an exciting new development. The emperor, in his divine wisdom, has just raised our Isthmian Games to a new level, designating them the Imperial and Caesarean Games, to honor the Imperial Dynasty and the goddess Roma. This is major—it means even more thousands will attend;

even more world-class athletes and artists will participate (with a new poetry contest this year); even more riches will flow into Corinthia; even more sacrifices will rise up to the gods; even more grain, wine, and sacrificed meat will be given out free, and—for those of us of noble standing—we'll be able to attend even more banquets. There, as we love to say, "we eat and drink and rise up to play"—and you know what that means.

Skeptical Time Traveler: Just what does it mean?

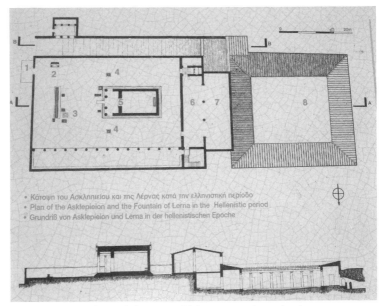

- Κάτοψη του Ασκληπιείου και της Λέρνας κατά την ελληνιστική περίοδο
- Plan of the Asklepieion and the Fountain of Lerna in the Hellenistic period
- Grundriß von Asklepieion und Lerna in der hellenistischen Epoche

Asclepieion floor plan and diagram, with banquet on lower level.

Babbius Italicus: Never mind; just use your imagination. Now I have a very special invitation for you. Later this evening the president of the games will host a reception for dignitaries and I'd like you to come as my guests.[3] It will be held in the banquet room of our magnificent health center, the Sanctuary of Aesclepius. You'll see firsthand what the elite of Corinth are like. If you'd excuse me now, I've got to bathe, get oiled, and get dressed. Hope to see you there.

Enthusiastic Time Traveler: Awesome! I'm so excited!

---

3. See appendix 1, "Arrogant Aristocrats in Action."

3

WHY DID PAUL WRITE 1 CORINTHIANS?

Sex, jealousy, love, divorce, prostitution, fancy dining, legal squabbles, life after death—the stuff Paul writes about in this letter would rival that of the wildest drama on television. What instructions should Christians obey, and what should we leave behind as no longer relevant? Unfortunately, we often misapply Paul's admonitions when we assume our own culture as the context, rather than that of ancient Corinth.

The setting we imagined in chapter 1 is based on clues from the letter itself and on passages from Acts 18 and 19.[1] They help us place Paul, Priscilla, Aquila, and Sosthenes in Ephesus, the city from which Paul and Sosthenes sent this letter. We know "Chloe's people" reported to Paul about quarrels and factions among the house churches Paul had helped plant several years earlier (1 Corinthians 1:11). We know that some Corinthian believers wrote to Paul with a number of questions about how to conduct themselves on specific cultural and social issues (1 Corinthians 7:1).

PAUL'S PROJECT

For Paul, more is at stake with the assemblies of Jesus-followers in Corinth than we have often realized. But recent scholarship helps us to recognize a new dimension

---

1. Acts 18:18-19; 19:1, 8-10

of his mission. It takes place in the context of a great empire whose positive image is increasingly challenged. Over the centuries historians have praised the "glory that was Rome." There is indeed much to admire about Rome's accomplishments: an unparalleled road system, architectural innovations like the Roman arch, cities supplied with fresh water, and even public health policies "more advanced than in European cities until the nineteenth century."[2]

What has often been overlooked, though, is the ruthlessness with which Rome conquered peoples and the cruel efficiency with which Roman rulers extracted wealth and services from some 90 percent of the population for the benefit of the top 10 percent—especially the super-rich top 2 percent. These 2 percent are the ancients who have left visible traces. It is they who have conveyed a positive image of the Roman Empire. The other 98 percent are mostly invisible. Writers of the privileged class rarely speak of them without scorn. One writer, the physician Galen, graphically describes the peasant class as reduced to a diet of "shoots and suckers of trees and bushes, and bulbs, and roots of unwholesome plants."[3] Meanwhile, those at the top, whether in provincial capitals like Corinth or Ephesus or Alexandria, or in Rome itself, lived well and ate well, thanks to well-functioning mechanisms of domination.

Paul is animated by an alternative vision: the kingdom of God, or the empire of God. It is the vision Jesus lived and died for and which was vindicated in his resurrection. Paul is totally convinced that this good news of God's coming reign is not only for Jews but for Gentiles as well. He understands that his calling is to plant vanguard communities in the Gentile world of the eastern Mediterranean. They are to oppose the oppressive and immoral ways of the imperial culture by organizing into assemblies of personal and collective resistance—for God's sake.

Our tour through Corinth with Babbius Italicus (chapter 2) and our visit to the Isthmian Games recep-

2. Engels, *Roman Corinth*, 79.
3. Cited in Elliott, *The Arrogance of Nations*, 183.

tion (appendix 1) showcase the thoroughly materialistic, power-obsessed imperial culture. No wonder small assemblies of Jesus-followers have questions about how to live their new faith. What inherited practices can we keep, and what should we give up? How should we live the alternative ways of the kingdom Jesus proclaimed in the midst of an alien world?

THE DRAMA BEHIND THE LETTERS

According to Acts 17–18, Paul arrives here fleeing persecution in Thessalonica to the north, followed by a lukewarm reception in Athens. He spends a year and a half in Corinth in 50–51 CE, sharing his message and building a community of believers in Jesus Christ—a gospel radically opposed to the "gospel" of the imperial religion. He probably rents a room in a densely populated tenement complex, working with fellow Jew Aquila and his wife, Priscilla, in their shop making tents and awnings (Acts 18:1-3). As he interacts with customers and bystanders and synagogue contacts, Paul proclaims his message of the crucified and risen Messiah.

After several house churches are established, Paul sails to Ephesus with Priscilla and Aquila, but leaves them there while he sails east, visiting his home church of Antioch and the mother church in Jerusalem. On the way back west he checks up on the churches he had previously planted in Galatia and Phrygia (Acts 18:18-23).

During Paul's absence in Ephesus, the Alexandrian Jew Apollos arrives in Ephesus and impresses everyone with his eloquence. After Priscilla and Aquila patch up the holes in his limited theology, they encourage Apollos to visit Corinth, and include a letter of recommendation (Acts 18:24-28). Apollos is a smash hit there as well, "publicly debating with the Jews" and "showing by the Scriptures that the Messiah is Jesus" (v 28). While Apollos is in Corinth, Paul returns to Ephesus (Acts 19:1). By the time the letter we call 1 Corinthians was written, both Paul and Apollos appear to be working in Ephesus or the surrounding area (1 Corinthians 16:12).

Much was happening in the region of Corinth that Paul left behind. In his aptly named book *After Paul Left*

Corinth, Bruce W. Winter details several events that took place between 51 and 54 CE. Each has consequences for Corinthian believers that will be noted in conjunction with particular parts of Paul's letter.

- The Isthmian Games have returned to Isthmia, the isthmus adjacent to Corinth that joins the Peloponnesus (southern Greece) with the rest of Achaia (Greece).

- A serious famine and grain shortage recurs.

- Kosher meat is withdrawn from sale in the Corinth meat market.

- Corinth is chosen as the site for a new province-wide emperor cult.

Much was happening in the house assemblies as well, and not all of the news Paul heard was good, as we saw in Chapter 1. Paul's response to all this is the letter we call 1 Corinthians.

A LONG AND PASSIONATE RELATIONSHIP

This is perhaps the most revealing letter Paul wrote. Along with 2 Corinthians, we have a remarkable window into the extended relationship Paul had with his churches in Corinth, more tempestuous and passionate than with those in any other city.

By the time he writes 1 Corinthians there are probably several house assemblies in the city itself and several more in the larger region called the Corinthia. For instance, we know that several miles east, Phoebe leads an assembly at Corinth's seaport of Cenchreae (Romans 16:1-2).

Furthermore, the detail with which Paul writes and the range of issues brought to his attention show us how deeply involved he was in the lives of these Corinthian believers. He feels free to scold them when it is necessary and gives lots of advice.

The two letters to the Corinthians in the New Testament refer to other (lost) letters Paul wrote to these churches, as well as visits made to Corinth by Paul himself and by his coworkers, Timothy and Titus. In 1 Corinthians

5:9, Paul refers to a previous letter in which he told them not to associate with sexually immoral persons. (A fragment of that may be found in 2 Corinthians 6:14–7:1.) But some Corinthians mistook Paul to mean that Jesus-followers should have nothing to do with the pagan world around them. So he clarifies that they should shun only those *within the church* who do not follow the moral practices of Jewish Scripture (1 Corinthians 5:10-13). Contemporary Christians are not the only people who misunderstand Paul!

See the epilogue for related events that follow the reception of 1 Corinthians.

A COLLECTION OF MESSY PROBLEMS

Here are the topics in the order in which Paul writes about them in 1 Corinthians:[4]

A. Paul responds to an oral report about factions and strife in Corinth—1:10–6:20

- Caesar's empire vs. Jesus' alternate, upside-down kingdom—1:10–3:4

- Unity between apostles Paul and Apollos—3:5–4:20

- Sexual misbehavior—5:1-13

- Lawsuits that go to public courts rather than to the church—6:1-8

- Visiting prostitutes—6:9-20

B. Paul answers questions from the Corinthians—7:1–11:1

- Marriage and Domestic Matters—7:1-40

  o Should one marry?

  o Should married people have sexual relations?

  o Should widows remarry?

---

4. This list is adapted from Barr, *New Testament Story* ,132–33.

- o Should a believer divorce an unbeliever?

- o How important is circumcision?

- o How can slaves live as Christ-believers?

- Food—8:1–11:1

  - o May we eat meat sacrificed to the gods and then sold in the market?

  - o Are we free to eat even if it offends others?

  - o May we eat in the home of an idolater?

  - o May we eat at public banquets?

C. Paul's further concerns on issues the Corinthians don't seem to "get"—11:2–15:58

- Conduct of worship—11:2–14:40

  - o What should we wear on our heads for worship?

  - o Why should we eat our suppers together?

  - o Which spiritual gifts are the most important?

  - o Should spiritual gifts be regulated during worship?

- Resurrection—15:1-58

  - o Will there be a bodily resurrection?

  - o With what sort of body are the dead raised?

- Collection—16:1-4

  - o How should it be taken up?

  - o When will Paul come for it?

GOD'S REIGN IN HEAVEN AND ON EARTH

Paul frames the main body of this letter (1:10–15:58) by references to Jesus' crucifixion (1:18-25) and resurrection (15:1-58). Because these events will ultimately affect human history, he says, a cruciform (cross-shaped) life of self-giving must characterize believers' witness today.

Paul's theology of life after death differs from common views in the western world. For example, many Christians today are concerned about what to believe and how to live so they can go to heaven when they die. Paul, however, never uses the phrase *going to heaven*. Instead, he retains the Jewish view that each person is an inseparable unity of body and soul. "Heaven," therefore, will take place on a physical earth (see Romans 8:18-25).

Paul sees ordinary, earthly life shaped by this living hope. This hope does not mean flying away from this world. Rather, it means actively living by the principles of God's kingdom so believers can be ready for Jesus' return to earth when he establishes God's complete reign here. The Lord's Prayer says it clearly: "Your kingdom come; your will be done *on earth* as it is in heaven." Thus the bulk of this letter comprises advice for how to live by these countercultural principles.

Such teaching, however, could threaten the power of the Roman government, for it ultimately means the end of all other earthly kingdoms. In contrast, the teaching that Christian believers go to heaven when they die would be no threat whatsoever to the imperial realm.

THE RUTHLESSNESS OF ROMAN RULE

The seriousness of Paul's mission is underscored by the brutality of Roman rule. When in 146 BCE, Corinth resisted Rome's dreams of empire, Rome sent land and naval forces to annihilate the city. General Mummius and his forces killed what men remained, sold women and children into slavery, looted Corinth's art treasures to decorate Rome, and left Corinth in ruins.[5]

- Terrifying examples of the Roman occupa-
  tion of Judea are well known to readers of the
  New Testament. In the birth story of Jesus in
  Matthew's Gospel, the Roman puppet-king

---

5. Cicero, traveling through the ruins of Corinth seventy years later, was deeply affected. See Engels, *Roman Corinth*, 16.

Herod is a jealous baby-killer. When Herod's son Philip is confronted by the nonviolent wilderness preacher John the Baptist announcing that a "kingdom of heaven" was "at hand" and headed by another "lord," Philip has him imprisoned and finally beheaded (Matthew 14:3, Mark 6:17; Luke 3:19-20). Then, one Passover week, this same "lord," another nonviolent but provocative Jewish troublemaker, is arrested, tortured, and executed by the governor Caesar appointed to control the unruly Judeans.

• Mass punishment is a particularly merciless form of Roman rule. In one instance when a slave killed his master, his four hundred other slaves were all killed in retaliation. When this was questioned, the Roman Senate, after debate, voted to endorse the punishment.[6]

Hidden messages of resistance and freedom

But the story is much more than one of Rome's ruthless rule. Religious faith is very often a catalyst for resistance, for the creation of "free space" in the midst of domination. When we think of resistance, we may think of violent action like a slave rebellion, a peasant uprising, or guerrilla warfare. But because the cost of forceful resistance is so enormous and the chances of success are so minimal—or because of a commitment to nonviolence—most resistance takes other forms. Most is hidden from public view, with little or no record of it. That is because either those dominated did not have access to the means to record their dissent, or their resistance has had to be disguised, to stay "below the radar."

Our Bible is remarkable as a rare collection of ancient writings that give voice to the dominated. In the Hebrew Bible, Moses leads slaves to freedom from the Egyptian Empire. The New Testament records the movement led by Jesus of Nazareth, an itinerant Jewish teacher. This movement sought to renew their people's covenantal

---

6. Glancy, *Slavery in Early Christianity*, 73.

relationship with the God they proclaimed as Creator
and Lord of all.

Keep in mind that any record of significant resistance
by the Jesus movement against the dominating system
would usually be hidden, that is, contained in coded or
ambiguous forms not easily recognizable by the powerful.
(Think of African-American slaves using quilts and spiri-
tuals to send signals about escaping to "free" territory.)
Let us look at some of the ways this "off the record" resistance to a domination system can be found in a variety of
forms.

- *Lament and complaint.* By crying out, the disin-
  herited give voice to the unbearable quality of their
  continued suffering. Think of the spiritual that was
  born out of slavery: "Nobody knows the trouble
  I've seen, nobody knows but Jesus." From their
  prayer book, the Psalms, the early believers recited
  such laments to express their pain and longing.

- *Joking and ridicule.* Which one of us hasn't done
  this a thousand times? Jesus does it too! He
  mockingly calls King Herod "that fox" (Luke
  13:32) and the Pharisees "whitewashed tombs"
  (Matthew 23:27). Paul of Tarsus ridicules the so-
  called "wise" who speak for the elite of Corinth,
  sarcastically asking, "Where's the one who
  thinks he's so smart?" (1 Corinthians 1:20).

- *Prophetic denunciation.* Remembering the harsh
  denunciations of the Hebrew prophets, the
  early believers cherish the traditions of John the
  Baptist and Jesus of Nazareth, who denounce
  religious elites as hypocrites and a "brood of
  vipers," and the rulers of the day as tyrants
  (Matthew 20:25).

- *Subversive stories.* Stories are told and retold of
  Jesus healing the sick, feeding multitudes, and
  driving out demons. The retelling of these stories
  undermines the image of the empire as meeting
  everyone's needs and offering good things to all.

The richest 2 percent would be confronted by frequent food shortages, endemic sickness, and rampant corruption.

- *Subversive claims.* Alongside were subversive claims about lordship and fatherhood. Jesus-followers resisted naming Caesar as Lord Caesar, son of a god. Instead, they praised the Lord Jesus, true Son of God, thus challenging the Roman regime. See examples in chapter 9.

- *Disguised protest action.* In Communist-controlled Eastern Europe, people would stage Greek plays about ancient tyrants, and perceptive people could identify them with the tyrants of their present regime. When Jesus rode into Jerusalem on a donkey, so common among peasants, he was mocking the imperial procession of the Roman legions with their commander riding proudly on a white horse. The praises from the Psalms which his followers shouted, defied the exalted rhetoric that extoled the empire.[7]

- *Creating an alternative vision of society.* Subjected peoples often imagine a different ordering of society. Such is Jesus' empire of God, a rule of justice and peace, surpassing even the golden age of King David. In this upside-down empire, the lowly will be lifted up, the hungry filled with good things, and the powerful brought down from their thrones (Luke 1:52-53).

- *The imagined destruction of the oppressor.* Echoing the Hebrew prophets, sometimes New Testament writers use apocalyptic language to imagine the violent destruction of the oppressing empire. It seems that those under domination are prone to imagine an end to their suffering in the form of God doing to their enemies what their enemies have done to them.

---

7. Borg and Crossan, *The Last Week*, 2–4.

As we enter into the lives of the early Corinthian believers, we want to pay attention both to the presence of the empire's ways and to the ways the believers resist the empire in disguised and hidden ways. The next chapter will summarize the values and social behaviors of pagan, imperial Corinth, which provide the backdrop for the house church we will simulate. How are these values and social structures radically different from or somewhat similar to Paul's vision of Jesus' new empire?

4

HONOR ABOVE ALL ELSE!
CORINTHIAN VALUES AND SOCIAL BEHAVIORS

We have seen the dominant culture of Corinth as we toured the city center with Babbius Italicus (chapter 2) and perhaps spent an evening with the notables (appendix 1). These are the values and social structures that surround the households of Chloe or Stephanas or Gaius. As Bruce W. Winter says of these early believers, "After becoming followers of Christ they did not automatically abandon the culturally accepted ways of doing things in Corinth."[1] We shall certainly see this throughout our simulation!

Let us summarize relevant aspects of this elite-driven society. First, the dominant spirit is one of *ruthless competition*. Richard Horsley states that first-century Corinth was developing "a reputation as the most competitive of all cities, even in economic matters, a city of unprincipled profit takers who would stop at nothing to outdo their rivals."[2] The Isthmian and Caesarian Games symbolize the city's fierce competitive spirit.

Second, Corinthians are *obsessed with rank and status*. This obsession penetrates all levels of society, not only

---

1. Winter, *After Paul Left Corinth*, x.
2. Horsley, *1 Corinthians*, 31. A brief but excellent description of the Corinthian context at the time of Paul's activity is found in Horsley, 22–33.

the tiny wealthy elite who scramble for *public honor* in
their city or for favor with the emperor. It extends all the
way down to the minor officials, to skilled and unskilled
freeborn laborers, to freed persons (formerly enslaved),
and to slaves. Roman Corinth was settled by freed persons, and their never-enslaved children and grandchildren
now want to forget the shame of their past.[3] They look
down on current freed persons, who in turn can despise
the slaves. Even slaves have a pecking order by the nature
of their skills and labor in house or field.

Third, Corinthians express *public piety.* The imperial cult (emperor worship) is combined with worship of
the Greco-Roman gods and goddesses. This cements the
power of Rome throughout her conquered territories and
increases the prestige of those who honor the emperor.
The elite are eager to gain respect and honor through
positions of religious leadership. They covet titles such as
priest or even high priest (*pontifex maximus*) of a shrine
to a particular deity, to the imperial family, or to Roma,
the personification of the empire. They conduct public
sacrifices and preside over special occasions. Imperial
religion is not a matter of personal faith, but of correct
performance of rites and rituals.

HONOR ABOVE ALL ELSE

The more successfully one competes, the more "honor"
one accrues. The more power, wealth, land, slaves, and
Corinthian bronzes, the better. Much desired are high
military posts and key civic offices, including city council
member, business manager, or mayor (there were always
two at a time). In Corinth, the most prestigious post
was president (*agonothetes*) of the Panhellenic Isthmian
Games, which ranked next in fame to the Olympian
Games.

Also necessary to the pursuit of honor is the *public display of one's power and domination.* This requires "conspicuous consumption." As one scholar puts it, "The elite
were distinctly marked by differences in dress, education,
and speech; the means of their travel; and even their diet.

---

3. Ibid., 31.

The homes and public buildings they built, their villas in the countryside, set them apart."[4] To maintain their dominance, elite men also expect lesser men to show submission to them on a day-to-day basis. Many of them walk around the city square each morning surrounded by their admiring clients. Some advertise their level of education by employing a resident Stoic or Epicurean philosopher as part of their household.

Another form of advertising one's position is to underwrite public events or donate public works—called "benefactions." This might include sponsoring a festival honoring a god or goddess, a birthday celebration of an imperial family member, or the donation of free grain to the masses in times of famine. Public works include donating a monument, erecting a public building or city gate, repairing a shrine, enlarging the baths, or paving a plaza.[5] While such good works may benefit the community, the motive is more to reap honors and attention from the authorities. The elite must project a clear sense of *entitlement and superiority*. They look with contempt on those who "do not count."[6] Surviving documents record cruel slander directed at, for instance, Jews, slaves, or Syrians. They disdain manual labor as beneath their dignity—which makes them heavily dependent on retainers and talented slaves.

What is "normal"?

Some of these values and practices may seem familiar to us, even normal. The privileged in every society breed similar attitudes. The Roman Empire was no worse than other empires or nations, and (save for the older Athenian

---

4. Heen, "Phil 2:6-11 and Resistance to Local Timocratic Rule," 129.

5. An inscription outside the ancient theater in Corinth indicates that one Erastus, the city treasurer, donated the paved plaza there; some scholars believe that this Erastus is the same person as the Erastus whose greetings Paul sends from Corinth to believers in Rome (Romans 16:23). For a recent discussion of the issue, see Friesen, "The Wrong Erastus," 231–56.

6. This sense of entitlement and disdain is expressed in our imaginary speech by Julius Spartiaticus in appendix 1, section III. It simply inverts Paul's declaration in 1 Corinthians 1:26-31.

"democracy") possibly the most "enlightened" up to that time. In whatever age, the elite are mimicked or envied by those who don't share their power or wealth. Most of the time their values are accepted as normal, especially by those who benefit.

In contrast to the elite, most residents of Corinth remain abysmally poor, living lives of quiet desperation as slaves, ex-slaves, or freeborn peasants. They can only view from afar, either with envy or disgust or disdain, the conspicuous consumption, social climbing, and crass materialism promoted by the tiny elite that we visited during our drama at the Sanctuary of Asclepius (see appendix 1). As Horsley summarizes: "Thus, amidst all the luxuries of Corinth, the people seemed uncultured and lacking in social graces, partly because the wealthy so grossly exploited the poor of the city. The recently founded city, full of uprooted people yet striving for the appearance of culture, had an atmosphere of spiritual emptiness, of hunger for status and security."[7]

In this skewed society, Paul is nurturing assemblies of Jesus-followers, urging them to follow the way of Jesus, not the ways of the "wise" and honorable elite.

In the next chapter, we begin creating the characters who make up the assembly of Jesus-followers led by a believer named Chloe. Combining clues in Paul's letter with the cultural context described above, we will use our educated imaginations to create this diverse house church. The members have a shared goal—but at the same time are split into different factions. Get ready to meet some early Corinthian believers!

---

7. Horsley, *1 Corinthians*, 31.

5

SLAVE OR FREE—WHICH WILL YOU BE?

CHARACTERS IN CHLOE'S HOUSE CHURCH

Slave or well born, poor or less poor, educated or not—in this chapter we travel down the unpaved side streets of Corinth. Here is Chloe's ground-floor apartment and shop in a tenement building, where Christian believers have been gathering for regular meals and worship.

In this chapter you will get to know the characters who will simulate the household of faith called "Chloe's people."[1] This assembly comprises a cross-section of the believers in Corinth and is rife with divisions. Several persons have reported this fact to Paul (1:11).

THE FACTIONS

There are four primary factions, each claiming to "belong" to a prominent mentor in the Jesus Movement (1:12):[2]

---

1. From evidence in Paul's letters, there are several house churches in and around Corinth: the household of Stephanas (1:16; 16:17); the household of Gaius, an early believer whom Paul baptized (1:14); "Chloe's people" (1:11); and the congregation led by Phoebe (Romans 16:1-2) at Corinth's port of Cenchreae. Gaius must have remained faithful to both Christ and Paul, for he later hosted Paul during the visit when he wrote to believers in Rome.

2. Scholars over the decades have pondered these divisions, debating whether some or all of these designations represent actual competing

- Those who belong to Paul

- Those of Apollos, a Christian teacher from Alexandria, Egypt (Acts 18:24-28)

- Those of Cephas (Aramaic for Peter), one of Jesus' original twelve

- Those of Christ alone—mostly women, mostly present or former slaves

Here is how we understand the character of these factions:

Those who belong to Paul: Chloe, (Phoebe), Fortunatus, Achaicus, Olympius, Trocmias. The Pauline faction is led by Chloe herself. She and her people care deeply about the unity and concord of the house church that originally met in her home, but they have run into seemingly insurmountable obstacles. The first four persons listed above were likely very close to Paul when he spent his initial eighteen months in Corinth. We can assume they were converted by him and absorbed the core of his teaching. They are inclined to support Paul's viewpoint on crucial issues and want to be faithful to his teaching.

Fortunatus and Achaicus recently visited Paul and their presence "refreshed his spirit" (16:16). Paul trusts them and wants others to "give recognition" to them, that is, to respect their judgment and their modeling of the faith (16:17-18). Phoebe is a patron of Paul's (Romans 16:2), but is not a regular part of Chloe's people—she has her own house church in Cenchreae. Paul trusts Phoebe to interpret his message and to reconcile people to his ways, even though they can be upsetting. She may well be reading his letter to Chloe's people.

Those who belong to Apollos: Erastus, Dionysia, Tertius, Valerius. Apollos, a teacher of the faith from the great

---

factions and, if so, exactly what they stand for. We believe they do represent actual factions (just as one might find in congregations or denominations today) and that thinking in these terms enhances our understanding of Paul's letter to the Corinthian house churches .

intellectual center of Alexandria in Egypt, came to Corinth after Paul's lengthy stay (Acts 18:24-28). Those in this faction are particularly impressed with his attractive appearance and eloquent speaking abilities and have attached themselves to him.[3] Typically, these Apollonians hold positions in civic government, not top positions by any means, but definitely responsible ones. They enjoy a status above most of Chloe's people, are more integrated into the imperial government, and have personal hopes of rising higher among the ranks of Corinthian civic leadership. They, unlike most in the house church, have some chance for upward mobility—something rare in the imperial system.

For the sake of public honor and prestige, these early believers like to do favors for the others—bringing special food to the *agape* meals, getting people jobs, hosting the meals in their larger apartments—in other words, bestowing patronage. They had wanted to do more for Paul when he was around, but he had resisted, which hurt their pride. Maybe on his next visit. . . .

They believe Apollos affirms both their membership in the body of believers and the responsible positions they hold in Corinth. To them, "resurrection" is more a metaphor than a historical reality. They also contend that the modest influence they have with important people they know may be needed to protect the fledgling house churches from persecution. The emperor's expulsion of the Jews from Rome a few years ago should be sufficient warning to be prepared.

Those who belong to Cephas: Deborah, Matthias, Enoch, Caulius. This group consists of Jews, like Deborah and Matthias, who were introduced to the gospel by the apostle Peter. As practicing Jews who observe Torah, the Mosaic Law, they respond to the thorough Jewishness of Peter's presentation of the good news. To them Jesus is the New Moses and the Messiah heralded by the great prophet Isaiah. They study the Jewish Scriptures diligently, looking for the connections to the crucified and

---

3. Crossan and Reed, *In Search of Paul*, 337.

risen Christ. To them Paul sometimes seems overly interested in Gentiles, rather than his own Jewish people. Last
year kosher meat was withdrawn from the Corinth meat
market. What's next? Is Corinth going to turn against the
Jews the way Emperor Claudius did?

*Those Belonging to Christ: Daphne, Alexandra,
Euphemia, Dorcas, Gaia.* These women share in common their experience as present or former slaves. Some
had been abandoned at birth to die, but were rescued and
raised as slaves. Most once held special devotion to the
goddesses Isis or Demeter, but found no release there from
the terrible psychic weight and material burden of their
station in life as slave, ex-slave, prostitute, or victim of
physical and emotional abuse.

But through their baptism into the body of Christ, they
experience a life-transformation in the radical baptismal
declaration: "in Christ there no longer is slave or free,
there is no longer male and female" (Galatians 3:28).
They feel part of a new creation, experiencing a rising
from the dead in their very lives. They embrace the gifts
of the Spirit in prophecy and tongues-speaking.

They also experience tension with Paul over the extent
of their newfound freedom in Christ. They have not by
any means given up on him; but they do believe Paul hasn't
yet fully understood the implications of being "in Christ."
He just needs another blinding flash from heaven, they
believe, to complete his vision of what being in Christ
means for gender relations. Dionysia and Deborah from
other factions have similar feelings about Paul's instructions on women's behavior.

THE HOUSE CHURCH OF CHLOE'S PEOPLE

Chloe's people, who will be our house church for this
reenactment, constitute a cross-section of the believers in
Corinth. The largest group is comprised of slaves, freed
slaves, and lower-class freed persons who have joined this
house fellowship because they live in the neighborhood,
just north of East Theater Street. Some work in the weaving and dyeing collective in Chloe's household. Some live in
slave quarters next to her small factory and house. Former

slaves and freed persons probably rent a tenement room in the neighborhood.

People are attracted by Chloe's compelling personal story, as well as the stories others have to tell. Phoebe is not a regular part of this fellowship, as she lives in Cenchreae. But she is a cousin and dear friend to Chloe and often visits, so Paul has asked her to read his letter to Chloe's people after sharing it with her own house church.

At first a small group gathered in Chloe's house for the meal and worship, but now they need a larger space, so Erastus, a patron of the Apollos faction, invited the group to his house—although this has added to the tension.

THE CHARACTERS

1. *Phoebe* (group leader should take this role)—"I'll never forget that fateful day I went to Paul's shop, the one he was sharing with Prisca and Aquila. I began a long journey from my lukewarm worship of Roman deities to the Jewish God Yahweh—and Yahweh's human representative, Jesus of Nazareth. I realized we don't have to bow down before the corrupt rulers of this age, but can honor the true Savior of the world.

"At first I resisted sharing meals and worship with my slaves and other lower-class people. But Paul's message about Jesus came through, and I ended up starting a church in my house. The stories of Jesus humbling himself and casting shame aside opened my eyes. I love the way God turns things upside down, as Paul always explains. I can't wait to see what God will do next. I continue to operate this shipping business I ran with Nektarios, my late husband. I'm so excited we've got this letter from Paul to help us with our divisions and unresolved issues."

2. *Chloe*—"My own life illustrates the incredible power of God to liberate, to heal, to restore. My husband, Olympius, and I were owners of a small farm on the outer edge of Corinth when he fell sick with an illness no one could identify. He was so weak he could not work, and there was more to do than our son and I could handle. Then the taxes doubled, we fell into debt, and the ruthless landowner went to court to take our property. Prayers for

Olympius's healing at the Asclepius sanctuary didn't seem to make a difference.

"Around that time, I heard Paul of Tarsus talking about a God who really cared for us. I asked Paul to pray for our family and things began to turn dramatically for the better. He and his believer friends invited us to keep coming to their shop for prayers and the *agape* meals. This saved our lives, because we might have starved otherwise, especially with the famine of 51. With food and these prayers, my husband began to recover. Now, he is well enough to put in half-days weaving, and we are in a position to help others who have fallen on hard times. It was through Paul that I met my distant cousin Phoebe, now my dearest friend. She has convinced me to take my concerns about the divisions among us to Paul."

3. *Erastus*—"I was brought up in a family of cobblers devoted to Venus, the Greek Aphrodite. I did well in my studies and eventually got a junior position with the city treasurer's office,[4] which has a lot of potential for moving up.[5] I was always attracted to the idea of one God, so I hung around the synagogue a lot, where I first met Paul. Later I met Apollos, who baptized me. I am rigorously honest in my duties, and I'm sometimes laughed at for not trying to skim off extra money for myself. I'm already seen as a little weird by the powers that be, so I'm hesitant to speak publicly of Jesus Christ as Lord. I'm afraid they'd see that as treason. So I go through the motions of attending to the cult of Augustus, while being, privately, an enthusiastic participant in Christian worship and generous in caring for the saints. On a personal note, I'm thirty now, and I'd love to get married and have a family."

4. *Dionysia*—"I grew up on a small farm outside of Corinth, and come from a freeborn Greek family of ath-

---

4. Romans 16:23.

5. Is the Erastus mentioned in Romans 16:23 the same one whose name is on a pavement stone from ancient Corinth? Probably not. See Friesen in "The Wrong Erastus," 231–56. The inscription refers to an Erastus of the second century, an upper-level city official.

letes. Some years ago, I myself won the women's 200-meter race both at the Isthmian Games and at the Asclepian Games in Epidaurus. My older sister Tryphosa also won this at both the Isthmian and Pythian Games, while our younger sister won the Isthmian two-horse war-chariot race.[6] Since retiring from competition, I've made a living coaching female athletes. I help the young women athletes to know that there's more to life than winning races.

"Now I am an organizer in the *agonothete*'s[7] office for women's events at the games. From my office in the Forum, I hobnob with a lot of important people and I enjoy this. As Apollos preached, there is incredible spiritual power in the resurrection of Christ and I want to live the resurrection now. I admit I am still sometimes tempted to visit the sanctuary of Hermes/Mercury, whose mysterious gifts of speed had made me such a sprinter."

5. *Daphne*—"The slave trader's wife who raised me told me they found me as a newborn on the town dump, screaming from hunger. They wanted me to be grateful to them for rescuing and feeding me. At the age of seven they sold me into a soldier's household, where I was raised as a slave mistress, then sold again into prostitution. I was miserable and turned to Demeter and Kore for solace.

"After some years when I was no longer sexually desirable, I was put on the auction block, where Chloe's people found me. Chloe bought me, took me in, gave me work to do, and treated me as one of God's children. They trained me as a nurse, with a special concern for women and children. Sometimes I assist the midwife Alexandra. Achaicus and I share a special relationship, and if both of us can win our freedom, we will legally marry. I feel so liberated in Christ and in worship. I love to pray and prophesy and speak in tongues. I'm not quite sure what Paul thinks of my sisters and me. And I admit, once in a while when

---

6. Dionysia is an historical figure and she and her sisters were in fact victorious in these races. See Murphy-O'Connor, *St. Paul's Corinth*, 14. The remainder of her biography is imagined.

7. The *agonothete* was president of the Isthmian Games, the most prestigious civic post in Corinth.

things are tough, I sneak up to the mountain to Demeter to say some prayers."

6. *Alexandra*—"I was just a small child when my family was kidnapped. Along with a hundred other natives of Crete, we were taken as slaves by the Roman legion that was quelling a disturbance we had nothing to do with. They wanted to "send a message" to any restless peoples. I grew up on a Corinthian trader's estate, where I showed special promise in caring for infants and pregnant women. I became an apprentice to the midwife, an older slave, and eventually became very much sought after as a midwife in my own right. My babies and mothers have a much better chance to survive than most. I was ultimately able to purchase my own freedom, even though it came at a stiff price.

"I used to be devoted to Demeter and the deified Octavia, Emperor Augustus's sister. But then I met a woman belonging to Christ, and she helped to change me. Still single, and now being so fervently devoted to the Messiah Jesus Christ, I plan to remain unmarried. I am very emotional about my faith, and my favorite saying of Jesus is, 'Come to me, all who labor and are heavy laden, and I will give you rest.'"[8]

7. *Fortunatus*—"I was born a slave in Chloe's father's household, and Chloe and I played together as little kids. She inherited me when her father died. When Paul had his shop just two streets over, we sometimes bartered our products for his awnings. That's how Chloe came to know Christ. As a thoughtful person, she began to experience a contradiction between her life "in Christ" and the ways of this passing age, especially wondering how she could be both a slave owner and a follower of Jesus.

"One day she told me that she was setting my common-law wife and me free. That act made me a follower too, and amazingly now we are one in Christ. Chloe recently trusted me to go with Stephanas and Achaicus to see Paul. What a once-in-a-lifetime opportunity! My wife

---

8. Matthew 11:28 RSV.

and I live above Chloe's shop. My wife does a lot of the dyeing, while I cast bronze objects for the leading maker of Corinthian bronzes, Claudius Optatus. I hate it when I have to cast those little figurines of Aphrodite and other so-called divinities."

8. *Deborah*—"When I was desperate, Chloe and Olympius took me into their household and trained me to design custom weavings. My husband had divorced me and nobody wanted anything to do with me, except to take advantage of me. Strangers raped me, which caused my fellow Jews to reject me. Chloe's intervention literally saved my life.

"Then disciples of the Jewish apostle Peter confirmed to me that in baptism God takes away the stains of our past. That has forever changed me. Christ is risen, and so am I. I was never a slave, but I do know what it feels like to be set free. I've become quite an independent thinker and will allow neither synagogue nor custom nor imperial decree, nor even Paul, to define who I am. I'm very devout and law-observant, and I pray daily the psalms I've memorized."

9. *Matthias*—"I came to Corinth after Emperor Claudius expelled us Jews from Rome six years ago. I escaped from my master, disguised myself as a woman, and fled with other Jewish refugees leaving Rome. That was the most harrowing experience! It did let me escape the sex slavery I was in as the "boy-toy" of my master in Rome, though. But I was panicked with fear about breaking the law and wracked with guilt about being sexually abused.

"When I met Cephas in his travels, I was so overwhelmed to know that baptism into Christ could wash away all the evil I was forced into. Every time we share the bread and wine, I feel reaffirmed in my new life here with Chloe's people. My work with the collective is to sell the cloth we make door to door or in the market square on market days. My worst fear is that my old owner will find me and torture me for running away. My greatest hope is to eventually marry a lovely young Jewish woman

I've met. I've been talking to her a lot about Jesus. I don't follow all the Jewish laws anymore but as much as possible I eat kosher. They don't sell kosher meat at the market anymore, but Caulius sneaks me a bit of goat now and then."

10. *Tertius*—"Though born a slave in nearby Argos, I was lucky because my master singled me out to be taught Greek and Latin along with his own children. My master donated an elaborate altar for sacrifices (for the temple of the imperial cult), and he received an appointment in the *duoviri's* (mayor's) office. Since I read and write much better than he does, he brought me with him as his scribe and secretary. I hope to purchase my freedom after the next Isthmian Games through extra transcribing and translating letters and wills. I love the pageantry and drama of the imperial religion—the incense, the robes, the smoke, the processions, the free food—all the grandeur of Mount Olympus and Rome right here in Corinth. I know these gods do not really exist so I don't take this stuff seriously—just patriotically. Jesus said, 'Give to the emperor the things that are the emperor's, and to God the things that are God's'[9] (though Paul once told me I had totally misinterpreted that line!)."

11. *Achaicus*—"I am jealous of Fortunatus. He was Chloe's slave and she set him free. I'm her slave, too, and she's not emancipated me. Then again, I didn't play with her as a child. But in Christ there is "no longer slave or free"![10] Chloe and her husband got me at age eighteen, just before Paul came. I'm well trained in math and good at managing the finances of the business. I was born before my parents were freed in Epidaurus, so I'm still a slave. At least here no one uses me for sex—that was awful. When we visited Paul I shared all my hopes with him, and I'm trusting he'll put in a good word for me with Chloe. When I hear Paul talk about Jesus and his healing, I think of Asclepius, god of healing whose huge sanctuary

---

9. Mark 12:17.
10. Galatians 3:28.

dominates my hometown Epidaurus. I think of Jesus as Asclepius come back in human form and I pray to both together—but I don't say anything to Paul about that!"

12. *Caulius*—"I am a follower of Cephas in Chloe's *ekklesia*. I come from the Berber people of Libya and converted to Judaism like many from my extended family. As an animal breeder, I was able to develop a thriving trade in hides and skins, even marketing some cattle to Rome's famous Forum Boarium. But when the Jews were expelled from Rome a few years ago, I moved to Corinth. On one hand, I can sell my hides and skins to the tentmaker apprentices that Paul, Priscilla, and Aquila had trained. On the other hand, since kosher meat can no longer be sold in the meat market, I sell it to observant Jews on the side and give some away to those left destitute and hungry by the present famine.

"As a Jew, I am attracted to what I have heard about Cephas, who is similar to this Paul that we hear about from Chloe. Our allegiance is to Yahweh and to his Law that has been revealed to us. Yet Cephas and Paul speak of Jesus as a prophet foretold by Isaiah himself. But is he the one and only Messiah, the Anointed One we have waited for? I also still believe that when I pray my head should be covered; it is a sign of submission to the one true God of the universe."[11]

13. *Euphemia*—"I am Erastus's slave and take care of his nice apartment, cook his meals, and sew his clothes. Ever since he was baptized by Apollos, he hasn't used me so much to satisfy his desires. I think he is conflicted, not quite knowing how to relate to me, especially since I got baptized too. I used to worship Isis because she was known to care about fidelity and women and children. But of course I could never afford the membership fees. In Christ, I find a freedom, a dignity that I never imagined, and I love to shout it out and praise the Almighty God who wants peace and justice and dignity for all. Erastus is a fine person—he's teaching me to read Latin—though he

---

11. Caulius's character was created by Hadley Jenner.

has some blind spots. I pray for God to liberate him from some old ways that still have a hold on him."

14. Valerius—"My great-grandfather was born a slave in Rome but was freed before being brought to Corinth as a colonist. My dad is a client of a city council member who got me a job working alongside Erastus in the city treasury. I'm lucky because it could lead to bigger things. Erastus, who has become my best friend, took me to hear Apollos's masterful rhetoric about Jesus Christ, and invited me to join Chloe's people. Apollos was so much more compelling than the Epicureans I loved to follow around. Christ followers really care about helping people and that's what I want to do. But I still like Epicurean philosophy; to me, Jesus is a philosopher, but the very best."

15. Enoch—"I teach all the children among Chloe's people, as well as those of several customers of the weaving shop. My master loans me to do this for them—for a hefty fee. Even though a slave, I am trained in Greek, Latin, Aramaic, and rhetoric. I am Jewish and know our history through the Septuagint Scriptures, so I know how God has been preparing for the revealing of his true Son. I once dabbled in Mithraism. I do have to assist my master with the household gods and the rites for the household gods. I hate that idol worship. The true God is Spirit. From Peter I learned what it means to be truly Jewish in these final days. I wish I were Chloe's and Olympius's slave instead."

16. Dorcas—"Our family of sharecroppers goes back even before Rome's destruction of Corinth. If we hadn't been out in the countryside, we'd never have escaped the brutality. We got along—barely—until the terrible drought a couple decades ago. I was a baby then, when the whole family was taken into slavery on account of our debts. After the children and I were freed at the death of our master, I married a widowed farmer and had five children. My husband died two years ago and we had nowhere to turn. The Jesus people saved the kids and me from starvation.

"My husband saw himself as a kind of philosopher-farmer, so as Stoics we never took the gods and the so-called 'divine' emperors seriously. But when I heard about Jesus, who was truly a divine teacher, God found me. Among Chloe's people I organize the *agape* meals where everybody gathers. Organizing dinner for fifteen or twenty people several times a week is a major task. Especially now during this famine, some of our people couldn't survive without these meals. I get such great fulfillment from this, though, because Christ is there with us in the meals. And there always seems to be enough for everybody—if everybody would wait their turn! I make everyone feel welcome, loved with the love of Jesus. After all, 'the last will be first, and the first will be last,' he taught.[12] And we have such a lively time in our worship!"

17. Olympius—"I am Chloe's husband, recovering from an awful illness and finally able to do some weaving again. I come from a long line of Greek peasant farmers around Corinth, going way back before the terrible destruction two hundred years ago. It's a tough existence, what with the Romans always trying to gobble up our tiny farms and olive groves. As farmers we always felt so dependent upon the whims of nature, so we served the harvest goddess Demeter.

"For myself I was also drawn to the Jews. I was what they called a 'God-fearer.' Their religion is so much simpler—you only have one god to relate to rather than a confusing lot of gods and goddesses. And the Jews are good people. They live by ethical laws that their God Yahweh had given them ages ago—not like the immoral gods and emperors. Don't lie, don't steal, don't kill, don't covet, don't commit adultery. Imagine doing business with people who didn't try to cheat you all the time! Of course you'd never be quite 'in' with the Jews—they are a bit standoffish—and men can't join without being circumcised, a wacky rule if ever I saw one. When we met Paul, though, my heart was warmed as he told about Jesus the Messiah whom God sent to set everything right and bring

---

12. Matthew 20:16.

the final victory—even in our lifetime. And he said to 'circumcise' our hearts."

18. *Trocmias*—"I live in my master Erastus's apartment on the edge of the Theater District, and I do his shopping, run errands, and help with his entertaining. As a handsome, very eligible man, he does a lot of entertaining. I also take care of his *lares*—his household divinities. I was captured last year in Galatia and brought in chains to the slave market in Corinth. I'm sixteen and so homesick for my family. We were all into the Isis cult and the emperors and found some meaning in that. But since Erastus has been taking me to fellowship with Chloe's people, my eyes are being opened to a Lord really worthy of worship. I can never worship an emperor again, after the way his legions humiliated us unarmed Galatians. I'm taking instruction from Fortunatus so I can be baptized and join the house church. One big thing, though, is that Erastus keeps wanting sex with me and I don't know what to do, because I'm his slave and slaves are supposed to do that."

> If you are reading this book by yourself, you may want to develop a character sketch from more than one faction. For maximum effect, we recommend choosing characters from different social classes—for example, from both the Apollos and Christ factions.

19. *Gaia*—"My family was captured during disturbances in Libya. I was sold to the household where I now live, but I never saw my own family again. At fifteen I had a son—born of rape by my master's friend—but he too was sold away from me. I dream about him all the time and wake up sobbing. I belong to a rich family here in Corinth, who work me from dawn to dusk. Besides preparing meals, my main responsibility is the large vegetable garden next to their kitchen. But our current drought has meant less produce, so I am often beaten when I have little to show for my effort.

"My family was Jewish, but I knew little about our history. Then I met Enoch, also a slave in this household.

He has taught me the laws of Moses. But he cannot teach me to read the Scriptures because I must work during daylight hours. And what slave can buy oil for a lamp to study by night?

"Although as slaves we cannot marry, we consider ourselves husband and wife and share a small tenement room with several other slaves. When I heard Paul teaching that in Messiah Jesus there is neither slave nor free, my heart leaped. Jesus came to let the oppressed go free, Paul said. That comes right from the prophet Isaiah, so Jesus must be the promised Messiah. But then why am I still a slave? Even Chloe has slaves, but hers are not covered in bruises, as I so often am. Paul preaches about this age coming to an end. Then will all slaves will be freed?"

DEVELOPING YOUR CORINTHIAN CHARACTER

Once you have identified your character, you can prepare to play that role in the simulation. Besides the information included above, you will find additional information in the following chapter. Some aspects will require your imagination. Make your character as complex and interesting as possible. We hope you enjoy stepping into a different personality and a different time!

6

ENGINES OF EXPLOITATION—
SLAVERY AND PATRONAGE

𐐒𐐒𐐒𐐒𐐒𐐒𐐒𐐒𐐒𐐒𐐒

In chapter 2 and appendix 1 we viewed Corinth and the Isthmian Games through the lenses of a tiny minority of aristocrats. Centuries later, North Americans developed a tradition of democracy, equality, and the dream of "upward social mobility"—moving from a lower to a higher social class if we work hard. In the United States, this dream has become quite tattered in recent years, as the gap between the rich and the middle classes grows ever wider. Opportunities to climb the socioeconomic ladder are diminishing as well.[1]

But empires like ancient Rome do not even promote *dreams* of upward social mobility. They value social stability and hierarchy above all else. Democracy in this context means chaos. Those few at the top of the ladder rule because they see themselves as inherently superior to

---

1. Most Americans today do not move into a higher socioeconomic class. In fact, by 2010 the poverty rate had climbed to a fifteen-year high of 14.7 percent, unemployment stood at nearly 10 percent, and real wages had been dropping since the 1980s rather than increasing. But because of our past heritage of democracy and economic opportunity, many Americans still hope that their children will be better off than they are. For an astute analysis, see Steele and Barlett, *The Betrayal of the American Dream*, 3–5.

those less privileged. The top *senatorial* class in the Roman Empire comprises about two-thousandths of one percent (.002%). The next order, *equestrians* (knights), probably amounts to less than a tenth of one percent (.1%).[2]

Under them are the lesser aristocracy and a small number of retainers—specialists to produce the luxury goods and services only the elite can afford.[3] The vast majority, at least 90 percent, lives at or below subsistence: slaves, freed slaves, and freepersons without Roman citizenship or civil rights. Many are native peoples the Romans have conquered or absorbed into the empire. Most of their energy would go to feeding their families and barely making ends meet.

The systems of slavery and patronage affect every person in the house churches of Corinth. How will they affect your character?

THE INSTITUTION OF SLAVERY

Nobles do not engage directly in commerce and industry; that is beneath their dignity. Ordinary labor is performed by those who have no other choice in order to survive— slaves, freed slaves, and the freeborn. Slavery is pervasive, since slaves are the economic backbone of the empire. Slavery is not based on race, as in our American past, but is no less demeaning and abusive. There are at least four ways persons become slaves:

- *Through capture as victims of war.* For example: a triumphal arch near the Coliseum in Rome honors the victorious general Titus in the frieze depicting humiliated Jewish slaves brought to Rome after the Jewish-Roman War of 66–70 CE.

- *Through breeding.* The child of a slave mother is also legally a slave. Children are often taken from slave mothers and raised by others, thus weakening family ties.[4] A male slave has no legal right to be a father to his own children.[5]

---

2. MacMullen, *Roman Social Relations: 50 B.C. to A.D. 284*, 88–89.
3. Rohrbaugh, "The Pre-Industrial City in Luke-Acts," 132.
4. Bradley, "On the Roman Slave Supply and Slavebreeding," 42–64.
5. Glancy, *Slavery in Early Christianity*, 9.

- *Through debt.* Some of the poor sell themselves or their own children into slavery in order to survive.

- *Through abandonment.* Unwanted infants, especially girls, are thrown out with the garbage, but are sometimes rescued by others and raised to be slaves.[6]

Understanding the true conditions of ancient slavery is difficult. A certain hierarchy exists among slaves. For example, some highly educated and aristocratic war captives fill important positions in the conquering government. (Think of Daniel and his three friends captured by the Babylonians in Daniel 1:1-7.) Some are skilled actors or gladiators. These are the ones we read about in the Greco-Roman literature—mostly written by the educated classes and through their eyes.

Until the 1980s, scholars of the Classical period tended to represent Greek or Roman slavery as rather benign, coinciding with their generally high opinion of these civilizations as advanced and humane. However, Orlando Patterson's 1982 sociological study, *Slavery as Social Death*, challenged this assumption by viewing slavery "from below." Patterson defined it as the "permanent, violent domination of dishonored persons torn from their birth families."[7] The power of the master over the slave is total. The slave can exercise no will of his or her own and lives perpetually in a state of dishonor.[8]

Building on these insights, New Testament scholars have used Patterson's lens to reread ancient Classical and Christian literature, inscriptions, legal codes, bills of sale, and other artifacts to fill out a more accurate picture of ancient slavery.[9] Jennifer A. Glancy's *Slavery in Early Christianity* stresses the perception of slaves as *bodies* to be used—presumably devoid of mind or individual will of

---

6. Saller, "Slavery and the Roman Family," 69–70. This list is also in Finger, 31.

7. Patterson, *Slavery and Social Death*, 13.

8. Ibid.

9. See *Slavery in Text and Interpretation*: Semeia 83/84. Allen Dwight Callahan, Richard A. Horsley, and Abraham Smith, guest eds.

their own. Slaves have no personal dignity or honor, so they can be raped at will by their owners. This indignity falls most heavily upon females and young boys.[10] Trying to persuade a male friend not to marry, the poet Juvenal sarcastically asks, "Isn't it better to sleep with a pretty boy?"[11] Such "pretty boys" are almost always slaves who are not permitted to resist.

On the auction block and in wills and property registers, slaves are called "the bodies" (*ta somata*). As surrogate bodies, slaves can stand in for their masters. If an owner gets behind in his dues to some association, a slave can stand in to receive the punishment of the owner, such as imprisonment, until he pays. Freeborn persons are allowed to speak to slaves as harshly as they please or even to physically abuse them, depending on what role they play in the household. Roman literature consistently suggests that slaves cannot not protect their bodies from a range of daily insults and intrusions.[12] The demeaning attitude of Babbius Italicus toward his slave is typical.

Although we usually think of slaves as male, Roger Bagnell thinks more slaves are female for two reasons. First, male slaves are often freed around the age of thirty, but females are kept for breeding purposes until they reach menopause in their late forties (unless they die first). Second, many more baby girls than boys are abandoned and raised as slaves.[13]

Even when loyal slaves are granted freedom and some civil rights after a number of years, they still have social and economic obligations to the former master as client to patron.[14] If a woman is freed and marries a husband, both he and her former owner have rights over her. If both husband and wife are former slaves of the same owner, the husband has no right to bring a complaint against his former owner.[15]

10. Glancy, *Slavery in Early Christianity*, 9.
11. *Juvenal: The Sixteen Satires*, trans. Peter Green, 127–28.
12. Ibid., 11–13.
13. Bagnell, "Missing Females in Roman Egypt," 121–38. Referred to in Glancy, *Slavery in Early Christianity*, 17.
14. Thomas Wiedemann, *Greek and Roman Slavery*, 3–4.
15. Glancy, *Slavery in Early Christianity*, 14.

PATRONAGE: THE PYRAMID OF INEQUALITY[16]

In North America, more and more money is being spent on political campaigns to influence voters to choose candidates who will then owe favors to the donors if they are elected. Even in our democracies with "one person, one vote," we know that wealthy and powerful people (and corporations) influence government far more than do the rest of us.[17]

But imagine if we eliminated voting altogether. Cut all government services designed to enhance the common good—transportation, education, police, etc.—or that operate as safety nets for those in poverty or victims of natural disasters. Instead, watch people struggle to find a slightly better-off relative or friend whom they can ask for help—for a price. Watch the increase in nepotism.[18] Watch massive pyramids of power and influence develop as clients seek patrons, and those patrons become clients of more powerful people or corporations. Nothing is free; those with less wealth or influence heap honor and compliments on their benefactors. Some persons or groups near the top of their pyramids manage to do very well. But the system itself is built on layers of inequality. Patrons do not allow clients to climb to their level of honor. A client is bound to his or her patron and must support the patron's interests, whether or not they coincide. Baptize this system as moral, and you have the structure of society in the Roman Empire.

Patronage is different from the three-layer sandwich of upper, middle, and lower classes that we are familiar with. Patronage means that clients cannot think of themselves independently of their patron. They cannot identify with

---

16. People in Spanish-speaking countries call this *clientelismo*, or *clientelism*, so as not to confuse it with the more positive meaning of patronage, such as "patron of the arts."

17. For example, the banking industry paid lobbyists $1.3 billion from 2009 to the first three months of 2010 to prevent further financial regulation, much of which relates to protecting consumers from being cheated by the financial industry. Rivlin, "The Billion-Dollar Bank Heist," *Newsweek*, July 18, 2011, 9–10.

18. *Nepotism*—favoritism shown by somebody in power to relatives and friends, especially in appointing them to good positions.

others in similar situations because they must be loyal to their patron in order to survive.[19] This explains why there are so few open revolts on the part of disadvantaged peoples.

The pyramids of power do not stop with aristocrats in a particular city but go all the way up to the emperor and the gods. Public animal sacrifice has a vertical dimension to promote peace between gods and humans. It also draws the community together horizontally as they eat a communal meal with the meat of the sacrificed animals.[20]

But this is not a meal of equality. Rather, it reinforces the pyramids of patronage. "Imagine," say Jonathan Reed and Dominic Crossan, "a downward spectrum of patrons from divinity, through royalty, priesthood, aristocracy, and citizens, to the free, the freed, the servile, and the enslaved. Think of sacrificial ritual as strengthening the bonds of loyalty among the many little pyramids built atop each other and made up of layers and layers of patrons and clients."[21]

PAUL'S VIEW OF PATRONAGE

Throughout our study, we will find many ways in which Paul interacts with and challenges patronage and social privilege. One important example is 1 Corinthians 9. In this chapter, Paul asserts the right of an apostle to be financially supported by those to whom he ministers (i.e., by patrons):

> Are you not my work in the Lord? . . . Do we not have the right to our food and drink? . . . Or is it only Barnabas and I who have no right to refrain from working for a living? Who plants a vineyard and does not eat any of its fruit? Or who tends a flock and does not get any of its milk? (9:2, 4, 6-7) . . . If we have sown spiritual good among you, is it too much if we reap your material benefits? If

---

19. Carney, *The Shape of the Past*, 94. A form of patron-client system is very much a part of Latin culture in South America today. The *patrón* promises (or is honor bound) to take care of you and in return you are loyal to him and faithfully follow his leadership.

20. Crossan and Reed, *In Search of Paul*, 297–98.

21. Ibid., 298.

others share this rightful claim on you, do we not
still more? (11-12a).

Nevertheless [insists Paul], we have not made
use of these rights, but we endure anything rather
than put an obstacle in the way of the gospel of
Christ. . . . I have made no use of any of these
rights, nor am I writing this so that they may be
applied in my case (12b, 15a).

Paul is so emphatic about this because he knows that
his support would come from the patrons at the top of
the house church pyramid. This would obligate him to
owe them more honor and respect than to the majority
of poorer, less-educated free workers, freed persons, and
especially slaves. He would be co-opted into the patronage system which stands in opposition to the good news
of equal inclusion offered through Christ. In order to
make the gospel "free of charge," he does not "make full
use of [his] rights in the gospel" (18).

Rather than tying himself to patrons, Paul is free to
identify with all kinds of people (19-23). He is free, but
he makes himself a slave. He becomes a Jew to win Jews;
he identifies with those who observe the law and those
who do not. He becomes weak and without privileges so
that he can win the weakest and most powerless. "I do
it all for the sake of the gospel so that I may share in its
blessings" (23).

By refusing patronage, Paul becomes a lower-class
manual laborer in his rented tent-making shop. This self-
emptying of privilege he sees as the very core of Jesus'
gospel. It is precisely what Jesus did by laying aside his
high status of being "in the form of a god."[22] He "took
the form of a slave" and humbled himself, even to death
by crucifixion—the depth of dishonor (Philippians 2:6-8).
This sheds light on 2 Corinthians 10–13, where Paul contrasts himself to the "super-apostles" (11:5), who apparently do accept patronage. This, he says, is tantamount to
proclaiming "another Jesus than the one we proclaimed"
and "a different gospel from the one you accepted" (11:4).

---

22. This phrase in Greek parallels a description of Augustus Caesar,
who was "in the form of a god." See chapter 3 above.

Paul closes the section of 1 Corinthians 9 with an image from the Isthmian Games (24-27). Just as an athlete must be supremely disciplined in order to win a prize, so Paul controls his own body "so that after proclaiming to others I myself should not be disqualified" (27). Paul knows that it would make life much easier to accept financial support from patrons. But this practice plays into the systemic inequality of life in the empire that does not represent the radical equality of Jesus' gospel. It is not easy to turn down money that you know you deserve, for the sake of a consistent, Christ-like message![23]

The gospel is thus most attractive to people with more dignity to gain and fewer privileges to lose. Jesus' gospel of equality and inclusion has given slaves in these house churches new confidence and a sense of worth that they do not receive elsewhere.

Tip: Preparing for the simulation. When reenacting Chloe's house church, only "those of Apollos" (and perhaps Chloe) play roles as its patrons. Divide the rest among lower-class freeborn persons, freed persons, and slaves. A pecking order surely exists here as well, but is much less pronounced.

---

23. Paul does not accept financial support from the Thessalonian church either, but for a different reason. In this church, everyone is poor, so Paul, Timothy, and Silvanus work as laborers to earn their own living (1 Thessalonians 2:9-13). He does accept gifts from poor believers in Philippi, Macedonia, but only for special needs in prison (Philippians 4:15-18) or to help relieve the famine in the Jerusalem church (2 Corinthians 8:1-4).

7

ISIS, ZEUS, OR CAESAR?

WHOM DO YOU WORSHIP?

When we lead a simulation such as this, people developing their characters sometimes ask, "How would I have heard about Christianity? Why should I become a Christian instead of belonging to another religion?"[1] To explain that, let's look at the religious scene in the first-century Roman Empire. When the gospel of Jesus Christ arrives, the stage is already crowded with religions. No strong antireligious feeling exists.

In some ways the North American religious environment, where we are free to choose our religion, is similar to the first century. Although it has God in its national anthem, Canada has become host to people of a variety of faiths—or no faith. The United States has a tacit "civil religion" represented by "In God We Trust" on coins and by Fourth of July speeches extolling the faith and wisdom of founding forefathers. Politicians, particularly in the U.S., sometimes proclaim their religious affinities to promote certain values or gain political advantage. In addition, there are variations of Christianity or many other religions. The only limitations are practices that interfere with others' freedom or defy the law or public morality.

---

1. Much of this chapter is adapted from chapter 5 in Finger, "Religions and Philosophies in Rome," *Roman House Churches for Today*: 54–62.

God-and-country in America. The Canadian penny omits any religious reference.

Such variety also exists in Rome and Corinth, but with significant differences. Today we assume there is only one God, but in the Greco-Roman world polytheism is dominant. Monotheism sometimes emerges in the form of the Great Mother or the Sun-God, but it is always in tension with polytheism. Throughout the empire, a person can worship a variety of deities and participate in as many religious rites as one can afford. Since the gods rule the cosmos and can help or harm, it is necessary to pay one's respects to as many as possible. One can never be too careful.

A second difference between ancient Rome and now is that, except in Judaism, ethical behavior is not necessarily related to religious practice. The philosophers, not the priests, teach ethics. The gods are essentially amoral—and quite often immoral.

Following are a few of the choices available in the first-century Roman Empire.

THE ROMAN PANTHEON

The poetry of Homer in the *Iliad* and the *Odyssey* around 700 BCE had shaped the picture of the Greek pantheon, with Zeus as father god and the subordinate gods and goddesses assuming specialized functions such as guarding marriage (Hera) and personifying nature (Artemis and Poseidon) or concepts like wisdom (Athena) or erotic love (Aphrodite). Later, Roman contact with Greeks has led to the assimilation of the Greek and Roman pantheons, with

Statue of Asclepius, god of healing. There are healing centers in many Greco-Roman cities, including Corinth. The priests care for sick people (those who can afford to pay) until they receive a healing dream from the god. Archaeological Museum at Epidaurus.

Zeus changing into Jupiter, Hera into Juno, and so on.[2] The god Apollo's son Asclepius was popular in both Greek and Roman contexts as a healer, spawning large healing centers run by his priests in many cities, including Corinth.

By the end of the Roman Republic in 31 BCE, this traditional religion had fallen into neglect. But Augustus, who ruled as the first emperor (27 BCE to CE 14), set about to rebuild shrines and renew religion—in effect, he inaugurated a religious revival. As a shrewd politician, he saw the value of promoting civil religion to unify the empire and strengthen his position as a benefactor of religion.[3] His successors follow this policy.

Worship of the Roman pantheon is observed by the upper classes who keep the traditions as symbolic of a comfortable, familiar way of life. As the empire embraces more and more peoples from outlying provinces, their local gods come along. They merge into the Roman pantheon; thus Isis can be identified with Venus or perhaps another goddess. New gods are also added to the pantheon in the form of previous emperors.

THE CULT OF THE EMPEROR

In Egypt divine kingship had been a long-established practice. Among the Greeks, in 324 BCE Alexander the Great demanded that people recognize his deity. Later Hellenistic rulers advertised their divinity with titles such

---

2. Ferguson, *The Religions of the Roman Empire*, 70–71.
3. Cary and Scullard, *A History of Rome Down to the Reign of Constantine*, 341–42.

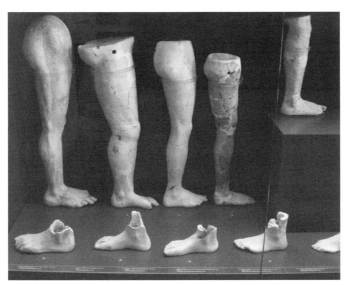

People bring a plaster copy of a body part that has been healed to the temple of the god Asclepius as a thank offering after he appears to the patient in a healing dream. Archaeological Museum of Ancient Corinth.

as "Savior" and "Benefactor."[4] Note how Jesus mocks their pretensions: "The kings of the Gentiles lord it over them; and those in authority over them are called benefactors (patrons). But not so with you" (Luke 22:25-28). John's Gospel directly repudiates other divine claims by calling Jesus "Savior."

The model of divine kingship was gradually adopted by ambitious Roman rulers. Augustus (27 BCE–14 CE) and most emperors who followed him did not directly declare themselves gods, although Augustus allowed temples to be built to himself—so long as his name was coupled with Roma, the personified spirit of Rome. Tiberius (14–37 CE) was also cautious and did not accept deification, though he was given such after his death. But he was followed by "Mad" Caligula (37–41), who demanded worship as a god. Claudius, the present emperor (41–54 CE), like Tiberius, has not asked for divine honors, nor refused them. Nero, ascending the throne soon after this letter (54–68 CE), will openly court them.

---

4. Ferguson, *The Religions of the Roman Empire*, 89.

Submission to the emperor cult is a civic duty, not a spiritual matter as we would understand it today. Its purpose is to inspire awe toward the emperor and to maintain the unity and domination of the empire. It expresses one's submission to the state in the guise of religious ritual, not unlike God-and-country theology today. However, the emperor cult could flex powerful muscles under threat. Caesar was Lord—and challenges to his lordship are not tolerated.

PERSONAL RELIGION—THE MYSTERIES

The state religion does not satisfy the emotional and religious needs of individuals. For that, many turn to the Mysteries, which come from the East and are quite popular in Corinth, where various mystery shrines have been established. The word *mystery* refers not to *mysticism* but to voluntary, secret, and personal initiations involved in a particular cult. The goal is to have a mind-changing experience of the sacred.[5] The Mysteries are diverse, but they have three common features: (1) a ritual of purification through which the initiate has to pass; (2) communion with some god or goddess; and (3) the promise of an afterlife of bliss for the faithful.[6]

Of the many mystery cults in the first-century empire, here are four of the most prominent, each of which figures in the past allegiance of our characters:

- *Eleusis.* This cult is based on the myth of Demeter searching for her daughter Kore (Persephone), whom Hades carried off to the underworld and who now returns for part of each year. Originally located in Athens, it has flourished since the sixth century BCE. Demeter is the goddess of the crops and fruitfulness, and her daughter Kore is the goddess of the underworld. Under threat of death, much of the cult's

---

5. Burkert, *Ancient Mystery Cults*, 11.

6. Ferguson, *The Religions of the Roman Empire*, 99. In a contrasting view, Burkert sees little emphasis on resurrection symbolism and more on good luck and a long life here and now; *Ancient Mystery Cults*, 23–24.

practices have never been divulged. In Roman times, Augustus himself became an initiate. An important sanctuary of Demeter and Kore is located in a majestic setting part way up the Acrocorinth, while the cult's chief sanctuary is located only forty miles from Corinth in Eleusis, very near Athens.[7]

- *Dionysus, or Bacchus,* is the god of wine and ecstasy; the phallus is his symbol. However, there is no chief sanctuary, so great variations of the cult exist. In earlier times, membership seems to have been restricted to women. Several times a year they would leave their families and severe gender roles to perform ecstatic rites in the countryside.[8] During first-century Rome, there are many Dionysian clubs, usually dependent on a wealthy founder. But initiations are kept secret. However, by this time more men are involved, and much of the sexual debauchery associated with Dionysian worship is committed by men with other men and young boys.[9]

> **A prayer to Isis** from the writer Apuleius, whose character Lucius prays "in a voice choked with sobs":
>
> "Holy and perpetual Savior of Humankind, you whose bountiful grace nourishes the whole world; whose heart turns towards all those in sorrow and tribulation as a mother's to her children; you who take no rest by night, no rest by day, but are always at hand to succor the distressed. . . . poor as I am, I will do as much as I can in my devotion to you; I will keep . . . the secret knowledge of your divinity locked deep in my heart."
> —*The Golden Ass, 11.24.6-25.6*

- *Isis* was originally an Egyptian goddess. In the myth, she searches for Osiris, her murdered,

---

7. This paragraph is based on Okland's detailed study, "Ceres, Kore, and Cultural Complexity," 199–229.
8. Kraemer, *Her Share of the Blessings: Women's Religions*, 39–43.
9. Ibid., 45.

dismembered husband. Isis finds and reassembles him, conceives by him, and gives birth to Horus. Isis and Osiris are often identified with Demeter and Dionysus. Both men and women join the cult of Isis, with some degree of gender equality. Women hold many offices in the cult. Isis protects marital fidelity and emphasizes the nuclear family. In this respect, Isis worship directly relates to the realities of many women's lives.[10] However, it is hard for poor persons to pay the initiation fees.

- *Mithras* is an old Indo-Iranian deity, known from the Bronze Age onward. The cult is held in underground grottoes, where small groups meet for initiations and for sacrificial meals in front of a painting or relief of Mithras slaying a bull. Only men are permitted, and the cult is popular among soldiers, merchants, and officials of the empire. Rites include the taurobolium, a ceremony drenching the initiate in the blood of a freshly slaughtered bull. Ritual meals are lavish, which indicates the poor are not welcome.

PHILOSOPHIES

The philosophers of the Greco-Roman age teach people to live in a hostile world—in other words, to be self-sufficient and not get too attached to the world. Two well-known philosophies of the first-century Roman Empire are Epicureanism and Stoicism.

- *Epicureanism* emphasizes reason and is critical of conventional religion and superstition. Epicureans believe in the gods but assume they are unconcerned with the world and neither reward nor punish. The soul is not immortal. The aim of life is pleasure, not in the hedonistic sense, but through cultivating friendships and avoiding pain. Ideally, Epicureanism renounces

---

10. Ibid., 74–78.

worldly ambition and pursuit of wealth, power, and fame. Peace of mind is attained by controlling desire and eliminating fear—especially fear of the gods and fear of death.[11]

- *Stoicism.* Stoics are pantheists: god is the totality of all things seen and unseen. Stoics have five arguments for god's existence: (1) humankind agrees that god exists; (2) someone has to be the highest in a scale of being; (3) a principle has to unify the universe; (4) the order in nature implies an ordering mind; and (5) piety, holiness, and wisdom imply the existence of god as their object.[12] Unlike Christianity, the Stoics believe that each soul is a spark of the divine, and after death the soul retains its individuality for a time but eventually is absorbed into the divine fire. The Stoics preach acceptance of one's state in life, be it slave or senator. Virtue lies in the attitude of the soul, not in action.[13] However, this makes their philosophy seem indifferent to the pain in the world.

JUDAISM

Judaism is a distinct and exclusive religion. There is only one God, Yahweh, and no other can be worshiped. Jews have sacred writings that give them a history going back over a thousand years—or to the beginning of creation. Unlike other religions, Judaism has a strong ethical emphasis derived from the laws of Moses. Besides the Ten Commandments, Jews observe other Mosaic laws, circumcising males (who are often valued more highly than females), observing the Sabbath, and heeding dietary restrictions.

Because they reject polytheism and emperor worship, Jews have an uncertain status in the culture. Sometimes they have political privileges, such as exemption from military conscription; sometimes they are discriminated

---

11. Ferguson, *The Religions of the Roman Empire*, 190–93.
12. Ibid, 193.
13. Ibid, 194.

against. Judaism's special appeal to Gentiles lies in its emphasis on the holiness of one God and on ethical living.

Choosing Jesus Christ

We now return to our question of how these first-generation Corinthians make their choice for Christ. We know how some Jews accepted Jesus as the fulfillment of the messianic hope recorded in their prophetic writings (*christos* is Greek for *anointed one, messiah*). We also know from the book of Acts that whenever Paul and his companions are rejected by Jews in a particular city, they preach to Gentiles.

Many of these Gentiles are already hanging around Jewish synagogues, often attracted by monotheism and by the Mosaic Law with its higher moral standards. They are called "God-fearers." More women than men embrace Judaism (such as Lydia in Acts 16). That is likely because circumcision is not an issue, and women are less involved in sociopolitical activities that demand outward homage to the emperor and his gods.

But Christianity is spreading beyond Gentiles with Jewish sympathies. Why? What is its appeal? There are at least five reasons:

- *First is Jesus Christ himself.* Compelling stories of his life, teachings, healings, death, resurrection, and ascension are told and retold. His Spirit had come upon the early disciples and is still available for baptized believers. His presence is known during the sharing of bread and wine in the Eucharist. Paul's own story is persuasive, since his life totally turned around through his encounter with the risen Jesus.

- *Second is the way of love revealed through the Christian communities (koinonia).* In these communities (ideally) everyone is accepted—Jew and Gentile, slave and free, women and men—on the same footing. This is quite novel in the status-conscious, male-dominated Greco-Roman world. Slaves and other poor are barred from mystery initiations because of the fees. Mithras does not admit women, while even the cult of Isis requires a male as high priest. Many find in their devotion to Jesus a sense of dignity that overcomes the life-long sense of worthlessness and degradation they have known as humiliated slaves or violated women, or as peasants, laborers, or artisans subject to abuse from those above them.

In the early Jesus Movement, women are not only accepted, but many become leaders, such as Chloe (1 Corinthians 1:11), Phoebe (Romans 16:1-2), Lydia (Acts 16:14-15, 40), Priscilla (Acts 18:1-3, 18), Nympha (Colossians 4:15), and the nine women in Romans 16. The poor and needy are cared for, babies thrown out to die are rescued and raised. Even the pagan Celsus, writing an indictment against Christianity in the second century, will declare that "where other mystery religions invite the pure and righteous, Christians invite crooks and simpletons, yes, and women and children, and the very teachers are wool-workers and cobblers and laundry-workers."[14] Indeed, our concept of universal democracy seems to have originated in early Christianity.

> **Tip: preparing for simulation.** If you are developing your character for a simulation, think through how you would have heard the good news about Jesus.

- *Third is the strength of conviction among Christians that cuts through the multitude of religious choices.* The reality of the Spirit's presence now, the certainty of the resurrection of the body, and the coming reign of Christ contrast strongly with the vague hints of future bliss promised by the Mysteries. Such good news enables many to endure persecution and mar-

---

14. Celsus in *True Doctrine*, preserved in quotations by the church father Origen in *Against Celsus.* Ferguson, *Religions of the Roman Empire*, 127.

tyrdom without flinching, which in turn attracts others to the faith.

• *Fourth is the strong ethical emphasis taken over from Judaism and further developed in the practice of* agape *love.* Jesus championed those on the margin and advocated for the "least among us" and proclaimed and enacted the mission of a kingdom of God where justice, righteousness, and reconciliation would prevail. Paul insists that this must be lived out in the Messianic communities he and others were founding.

• *Fifth is the interconnected nature of people's lives.* Church growth is often facilitated by the close quarters in which people live in Greco-Roman cities. They spend much of their lives outdoors and rub shoulders on the street, at the baths, and in their shops and packed tenement houses.

PART II

THE PLAY BEGINS!
REENACTING CHLOE'S
HOUSE CHURCH

From here on, each chapter of this book will lead your simulation group through a portion of Paul's letter. We assume that members of the group have become familiar with the background of chapters 1 to 7 and, if possible, acted out the gathering of Corinth's elite (appendix 1). All chapters will be structured in a similar way. The main idea of the passage will be introduced, followed by a section called "Understanding the Background." Participants will then prepare themselves for the simulation. A chosen reader will read (or perform!) the text from the printed adaptation.

The simulation continues as house church members stay in character and discuss the printed questions or other relevant ones that come to mind. At this point they should refer to the biblical text, preferably the printed adaptation, NRSV, or CEB.[1] (Even though most Corinthians could not read, their oral memory skills were far better trained than ours today.) The leader will close the simula-

1. Common English Bible (2011)

tion in time for a period of debriefing and a discussion of contemporary applications.[2]

This first simulation (chapter 8) is somewhat unusual in that it will focus more on ancient writing and speaking *styles* than on theological and ethical content.

---

2. For more details, see the Leader's Guide in appendix 2.

8

HIDDEN PERSUASIONS IN PAUL'S GREETING

1 Corinthians 1:1-9

It's time! Welcome to the first-century stage we have created! On this warm summer evening of 54 CE, we are gathering with Chloe's house on one of Corinth's side streets. Two of our members, Fortunatus and Achaicus, have just returned from Ephesus, along with Stephanas and Julia, hosts of a different assembly. Chloe has arranged for a good oral reader to present the letter that Paul has sent along. This letter is arousing great curiosity throughout the house churches in Corinth.[1]

Understanding the background

How Paul adapts the Greco-Roman letter form. Many of us today communicate instantly by phone, email, Facebook, or texting. Personal handwritten letters sent by "snail mail" are nearly extinct. By contrast, letters sent in Paul's day were written on papyrus and carried, sometimes for weeks, by a trusted traveler or paid courier. Only the Roman military used an express postal system.

---

1. Paul uses the Greek word *ekklesia* which we usually translate "church." It originally meant a civic assembly in Greek government. All such Jesus-assemblies met in houses or tenements, so we call them "house churches."

Since most people could not write and had to pay a scribe, most Greco-Roman letters were brief, sending only greetings and necessary news. Paul, however, adapted the letter form in his unique way.

In typical Greek or Roman letters, the opening, or salutation, involved three parts: (1) identification of sender and addressee; (2) expression of greetings; and (3) a wish for good health and prayer to a deity for the recipient.

In all his letters, Paul includes the first two parts, although he changes the word for "greetings" (*chairein* in Greek) to "grace (*charis*) to you and peace" (*eirēnē*, the Greek form of the Hebrew greeting *shalom*).[2]

Then, instead of a wish for good health, Paul includes a *thanksgiving*.[3] He thanks God for particular characteristics of the church he is addressing, usually for their work in the gospel of Messiah Jesus. Then he hints at themes he intends to discuss in the body of the letter, often ending with their common hope in the return of the Lord. This three-part introduction will be our text for today's simulation.

There are two other differences between typical Greco-Roman letters and those of Paul. First, Paul does not write to individuals. He addresses an entire church or group of churches in one city or region.[4] The letter would then be circulated to all the house churches in that city. Second, Paul's letters are much longer and deal with substantial topics. Because they are meant to be read aloud in an assembly of believers, the main body of each letter is structured as an oral speech meant to persuade the audience through the use of rhetoric.

What is rhetoric? In the ancient world, rhetoric was the art of persuasive speech-making. It was a major subject

---

2. Cosby, *Apostle on the Edge*, 93. This information is found in many commentaries and other books on Paul's letters.

3. Note, however, that Galatians does not have a thanksgiving. In that letter Paul is very angry and disappointed about what is happening in these churches, so he omits it entirely.

4. This is true among all of the "undisputed" letters of Paul. Authorship of those sent to Timothy and Titus in our New Testament is disputed among scholars and may have been written a generation or so later.

taught to sons of the wealthy and well born. Since Paul's use of rhetoric can be quite sophisticated, he must have had a good education growing up in Tarsus.

Depending on his purposes, Paul uses different rhetorical styles in his letters. Most of 1 Corinthians is advice-giving, since people have reported problems to Paul and asked for help. He also uses praise and blame, as well as sarcasm. A standard rhetorical technique is imitation. A speaker uses himself as a model for some reason of moral character.[5] We see this in 1 Corinthians 9 and 11:1, where Paul uses his own example of renouncing financial support to call for elite believers to give up certain privileges that undermine unity.

Paul's overarching concern throughout this letter is the divisions and factions that have arisen among the believers in Corinth. This is a common theme among the elite pagan writers as well, and Paul uses the same terms they do when talking about unity and peace in Greek or Roman society.[6]

Paul's thesis for his entire letter is found in 1:10: "My brothers and sisters, I am intensely concerned that all of you agree with and get along with each other. Using Jesus' authority, I plead with you to join together in the same mind and with the same purpose" (authors' translation). This problem of factions pervades not only chapters 1–4 but chapters 5–16 as well.[7] Paul's rhetorical style thus shows his passion for unity on behalf of his overriding purpose—to establish vanguard communities of God's empire.

What kind of unity? Two different visions. But how does Paul's concern for unity and peace compare with contemporary Roman speeches? All upper-class politicians want peace! But the most prominent theme in speeches from the early empire is "peace, established and maintained by the emperor throughout the whole world."[8]

---

5. Horsley, *1 Corinthians*, 43.
6. See Mitchell, *Paul and the Rhetoric of Reconciliation*.
7. Ibid., 65–67.
8. Horsley, "Rhetoric and Empire—and 1 Corinthians," *Paul and Politics*, 72–102.

Unlike Paul (as we shall see throughout his letter), Roman orators have a stake in the established social order. The elite know that they benefit from exploiting the lower classes in their economy. They want to convince them to remain in their present positions. Besides alluding to the threat of force, orators sometimes shame the masses as criminals if they even harbor thoughts of resisting.

Although the Greeks had tried a limited democracy among male citizens for the past several centuries, the Roman aristocrats detest democracy. Under imperial Roman rule, they have gained control of the Greek city assemblies, or simply abolished them. They have destroyed the Greek law courts and established a property requirement for holding public office. Their own Roman courts have become instruments of the wealthy and powerful. Thus, as democracy was declining, the elite relied ever more heavily on rhetoric to claim the loyalty of ordinary people.[9]

Statue of Caesar Augustus as Lord of the Empire.

Hidden messages on "fatherhood" and "lordship." In his greeting to the Corinthians Paul blesses them with "Grace . . . and peace from God our Father and the Lord Jesus Christ" (1:3). This is a scarcely disguised expression of treason. In imperial religion, overarching fatherhood and lordship belong only to the gods and goddesses and their representatives on earth, Caesar Augustus and his successors. "Father of the Fatherland" is one of Augustus' imperial titles, but for Jesus-followers, Caesar is neither their father, nor the land his land. Rather, for them these belong only to God the Creator, maker of heaven and earth.

---

9. Ibid., 79–80.

Shortly before Jesus was born, provincial rulers declared "the birthday of the most divine Caesar" as "the beginning of life and living," and named Caesar as the "savior" whose good deeds outshine those of any other ruler, past or future. His birth, they proposed, should be celebrated by making the first day of every year to fall on the birthday of Caesar Augustus (September 23). Imagine, from such a perspective, how suspect is Paul's reference to the transcendent grace and peace that flow from the true "God our Father" and the true "Lord Jesus Christ."[10]

Why does this letter have two authors? This letter comes from Paul and "our brother Sosthenes." We know little about Sosthenes except that he is a former official of the Jewish synagogue in Corinth (Acts 18:12-17). He must now be working with Paul in Ephesus. Sosthenes' inclusion in the salutation is no accident—he helps connect Paul to the Corinthian believers and may have been his scribe.

Preparing for the simulation

Since this is the first simulation, expect some awkwardness and humor! It takes awhile to "get into" character.

First meet in factions and discuss your group's character, beliefs, and persuasions. How is your group different from the other factions? What is wrong with them that they can't agree with you? How serious do you think is the strife—or is it not serious? Not having heard Paul's letter yet, are you mentally prepared to support Paul or not?

Then convene in the large group, but sit together by factions. Each person should wear a name tag and briefly introduce themselves by name, ethnicity, religious background, social status, and one factoid that helps others remember who she or he is.

Reader performs 1 Corinthians 1:1-9:

> *This letter is from Paul, an apostle sent by Messiah Jesus through the will of God. It comes also from our brother Sosthenes. We are writing to the church of*

10. Crossan and Reed, *In Search of Paul,* 239–40.

God in Corinth—to those who are made holy through the Messiah. Like all those in every place who name Jesus as our Lord, you also are called to be holy, set apart from polytheistic Roman society. May divine favor and peace from our Father God and the Lord Jesus rest upon you. (1:1-3)

I often thank my God for you because God's grace comes to you through Jesus Christ. You were made rich through him in everything, in all kinds of speaking and understanding. Indeed, you don't lack any spiritual gift as you wait for our Lord Jesus to be fully revealed. He will undergird you to the end, so that there will be no charges against you on the day of our Lord Jesus. The faithful God called you to be partners with his Son. (4-9)

RESPONDING TO PAUL'S LETTER AS A HOUSE CHURCH

Each person should now freely refer to the written text. Use the following questions to stimulate discussion in your group and feel free to raise pertinent issues of your own. The group may want to designate a leader to begin the conversation.

1. What memories does each of you have of Paul? Why does he remind you he was called to be an apostle? Do you remember what he taught?
2. Given the divisions within and among the house churches in Corinth, how do you relate to Paul's opening words in 1:1-9? Is he laying it on too thick? Do you feel and act like you are a sanctified saint (v. 2)? Or is he being sarcastic?
3. If this thanksgiving includes hints of topics Paul will discuss later, what might they be? Which of these topics are sore spots?

DEBRIEFING AND APPLYING

Spend a little time analyzing the simulation. How comfortable or awkward did you feel? What do you want to say now that you couldn't while you were in Corinth? Are there places where you disagree with Paul or would like to challenge him?

A vital part of our study of 1 Corinthians is what it can mean today, given our different situations. What parallels might we draw for our church life today?

1. What spiritual gifts characterize your home congregation or small group? If a church overseer wrote a letter to you, what spiritual gifts might be mentioned that characterize it? What might an overseer be grateful for?
2. What forms of persuasive rhetoric are typically used in the sermons you hear?
3. In our culture today, how is the media used to persuade and affect our thinking and behavior? What hidden messages can we identify?

9

THE WISDOM OF THE WORLD VERSUS THE WISDOM OF GOD

1 CORINTHIANS 1:10–3:4

Divisions, parties, factions—they are so much a part of life. On the international level, we have industrial nations and developing countries. In the United Nations, five nations are permanent members of the Security Council, and over a hundred are not. Some, like India, believe they belong there too. In our American political process, we have two major parties and a number of smaller ones. Even in our families, we sometimes divide up according to different interests and histories.

Often you find different factions or parties in a church congregation as well. Some have to do with liberal/conservative divisions, others with allegiance to a particular pastor. Some concern finances and facilities: Can we afford an addition to the church building? Should we house a homeless shelter? What music should be used in worship? Does the nation's flag belong in the church sanctuary? Differences can separate long-time members from new ones, those better off from those less well off, or even women from men.

Here in Corinth serious divisions have developed within and among the house fellowships in the three years since Paul brought the message about Jesus. In addressing his letter to these earliest Jesus-followers, Paul gives us a unique window into their life together. As you reenact the reception of Paul's letter, each of you is part of a faction. How do your character and your faction hear these first chapters? Does Paul identify with your faction—or not? Later you will discuss what clues we can gather for dealing with divisions and factions in our time.

UNDERSTANDING THE BACKGROUND

"The message of the cross" (1:18) and "Christ crucified" (1:23). In an attempt to bring the factions together, Paul immediately plunges into the basic—and most radical— aspect of his message. According to Roman cultural values, it is counterintuitive and upside down. The believers are following a Messiah who has been shamefully crucified by "the rulers of this age" (2:8)—but these rulers are the same as the very ones some of you are sucking up to! Throughout these two chapters, Paul tries to shock some of you out of your old habits of thinking and acting. Worldly wisdom is at cross purposes with the wisdom of God.

References to Jesus' cross in this particular text do not address the common teaching that "Jesus died in our place so we can be saved."[1] Death by crucifixion is so cruel and humiliating it is reserved only for runaway slaves, criminals, and revolutionaries. Paul is speaking of Jesus' willingness to challenge the powers and lay down his life and his divine honor to become an object of derision and shame. This is the Messiah Paul follows. Now he calls his churches to identify with Jesus in his self-emptying and to forsake climbing the Corinthian ladder of honor and status.

"Not many of you are wise, powerful, and well-born" (1:26). Paul's view of the upside-down empire of God is illustrated by the composition of the Corinthian house churches: most of you believers are "low and despised in the world" (v. 28). But this reversal of honor—which

---

1. Theologians call this "substitutionary atonement."

looks like foolishness—is wiser than human wisdom because God will use what is weak to bring the strong to nothing (vv. 27-28).

Resisting "this present age" (2:6) and its media monopoly. In chapter 3 we discussed an apocalyptic world view— how in times of political and economic domination, Jewish longing increases for the coming reign of God. Paul wants to remind both Jews and Gentiles that they are called to begin living out the justice and peace of this empire of God right now. In fact, the ability to imagine a different outcome in the future is one of the ways in which oppressed peoples can resist their domination.

Paul knows that this upside-down wisdom is "not a wisdom of this age or of the rulers of this age" (2:6), who assume they will always be in charge. The spirit of evil—called Satan or the devil or the strong man—has great power and holds captive the earthly powers that be. But in their alternate lifestyle, Jesus-followers have begun to strip "the rulers of this age" of their author-ity—from Emperor Claudius and the Roman pantheon all the way down the patronage pyramid of exploitation and inequality. These rulers belong to "the present age" which, whether they know it or not, is passing away.

This conviction is both countercultural and treasonous to the empire, and an insult to the gods. They will seek retribution. And because this narrative of the doomed present age is so out of synch with Greco-Roman think-ing, the believing community must constantly retell the story of God's history of liberation from alien empires. Because the imperial religion is such a media monopoly, they must constantly reinforce each other's faith in this unseen reality.

This omnipresent ideology and its values confront the eye with imposing temples and shrines, with their vaulting columns, carved pediments, and larger-than-life statues of gods and the imperial family. If you can read, your eyes cannot avoid innumerable stone inscriptions lauding the deeds of heroes, gods, and emperors.

For the masses who cannot read, the ear is filled with poetry, music, and rhetoric. The imperial religion enters the body through smell of incense and burning animal sacrifices, the smoke carrying the people's devotion to the heavens. And your hands hold coins that carry the core message in images of emperors and gods and symbols of victory, power, and glory.

Ruins of the temple of the god Apollo. This was 700 years old when Paul arrived in 50 CE.

How the Apollonians interpret Apollos's teaching. Apollos is a teacher and evangelist who follows Paul in planting Christ-assemblies in Corinth. Paul describes their relationship as "I planted, Apollos watered, but God gave the growth" (3:5). This suggests that Paul trusts Apollos in communicating the gospel and nurturing the community of believers.

We believe, however, that while the essence of their teaching is the same, "those of Apollos" exaggerate some nuances in Apollos's teaching to justify their practice of the new faith. Apollos hails from Alexandria (Acts 18:24-28), where the great Jewish thinker Philo has been teaching a philosophical Judaism, without the sense that God is about to overturn the existing order. Following Philo, Apollos seeks to communicate the new gospel teaching using concepts of "wisdom" and philosophy which were familiar to educated Corinthians from Greek philosophical traditions.[2]

You who "belong to Apollos" are influenced by your relatively privileged positions. You downplay the in-

---

2. In *1 Corinthians*, Horsley argues forcefully for the impact of the Philo wisdom tradition on Apollos's teaching. While we agree that Apollos's presentation may be using some of Philo's style and language for communication purposes (as theologians of all ages have used current philosophical and intellectual categories), we do not join Horsley in believing Apollos is preaching an alternate gospel. Rather, as we explain, we believe the opportunistic "Apollonians" use a selective take on Apollos's teaching to justify their elitism and their compromises with aristocratic values.

breaking of God's reign into history. Rather, the ills and injustices of the world are to be overcome through reorienting one's inner thinking and being to God. You emphasize Jesus as a teacher of life-transforming wisdom rather than focusing on his humiliation and execution. For you, Jesus' wisdom embodies both Hebrew wisdom *and* the Greek tradition of sages from Socrates to the Stoics.

This interpretation is very selective and not faithful to the fullness of Apollos's proclamation. It attracts you Corinthian believers who have much to lose in terms of socioeconomic status and perhaps much to gain as you pursue the career path of the moderately privileged. You think you have reconciled the ways of Corinth with the ways of Jesus. You are intoxicated with a new level of personal freedom in Christ. As we shall see later, you disregard not only Jewish laws, but even certain Roman laws and customs you think should no longer apply.

Overall, "this present age" doesn't appear so bad to you privileged Apollonians. And with your means and influence, you receive honor as patrons to others less fortunate in the house churches.

PREPARING FOR THE SIMULATION

Those of Apollos and those of Paul—After hearing 1:10 to 3:4, your dialogue should highlight the serious divisions of opinion between your factions. If anything, exaggerate the differences to reflect these divisions as clearly as possible. At this stage of the role-play, factions should be polarized!

Those of Cephas/Peter—Hearing this text, you will tend to defend Paul, for you retain Jewish moral standards. You long for the overthrow of the Roman oppressors, just as God had rescued the Israelites of old from slavery in Egypt and from captivity by the Babylonians.

Those of Christ—you Corinthian women prophets are of divided mind. You do not at all identify with the privileged position of the Apollonians. However, Jesus' gospel has freed you from conventional moral condemnations because of your lives as slaves, as "unclean" women raped and beaten by masters and husbands. Having lived lives of extreme deprivation and suffering, you are focused more on life in the resurrected Christ than on the crucified Christ.

Phoebe or another reader performs 1 Corinthians 1:10–3:4:

HAS CHRIST BEEN TORN INTO PIECES?

My brothers and sisters, I am intensely concerned that all of you agree with and get along with each other. Using Jesus' authority, I plead with you to join together in the same mind and with the same purpose. Chloe's people have reported to me that you are quarreling. I hear that each of you is saying, "I belong to Paul," or "I belong to Apollos," or I belong to Cephas," or "I belong to Christ himself." (1:10-12)

I ask you, has Christ been torn into pieces? Or were you baptized into the name of Paul? I'm grateful I baptized none of you—except Crispus and Gaius—so that none of you can say that you were baptized in my name. (Come to think of it, I did baptize the household of Stephanas, but I don't remember anyone else.) (13-16)

The Messiah did not send me to gather disciples for myself, but to proclaim his good news. And he didn't send me to use any fancy rhetoric, so that none of the power of his cross would be smoothed over. (17)

THE WISDOM OF THE WORLD—OR A CRUCIFIED CHRIST?

What we say about the cross sounds foolish to those heading toward destruction, but to us who are on the road to salvation, it actually shows God's power. (That's what Scripture says: "I will destroy the wisdom of the wise, and bring to nothing the learning of the intelligent.") Don't you see how God's ironic use of the cross has shown up the foolishness of the world's wisdom? (18-20)

So while the Jews ask for miracles and the Greeks insist on wisdom, we are proclaiming a crucified Christ! It sounds scandalous to Jews and like utter nonsense to Gentiles. But for those of us who are being called, whether Jews or Greeks, Jesus is the power and wisdom of God! God's "foolishness" is wiser than human wisdom, and God's "weakness" is stronger than human strength. (22-25)

GOD'S GREAT REVOLUTION

Consider your own situations, sisters and brothers. By ordinary human standards, not many of you were wise or wealthy or influential. Very few of you are from high-society families. But God chose what the world considers foolish to bring shame on those the world calls "wise." God chose those the world calls "weak" to show up those called "strong." God chose what the world deems insignificant and contemptible, mere "nobodies," to overthrow the existing order. (26-28)

Not one person has anything to brag about in the presence of God. Who and what you are is a gift from God through Messiah Jesus. He has become God's wisdom and righteousness and holiness and freedom for us, in order that, as it is written in the Bible, "Let anyone who boasts boast in the Lord." (29-31)

When I came to you, brothers and sisters, I did not come with clever words or high-sounding philosophy. During my time with you, the only knowledge I claimed was about Jesus Christ as one crucified. I felt shaky and nervous, but in that way you would not trust human accomplishments but instead trust the power of God. (2:1-5)

THE RULERS OF THIS WORLD ARE DOOMED

But what we speak sounds wise to those who are truly mature. The wisdom of popular culture or from today's leaders will eventually be reduced to nothing.

We speak God's wisdom, now secret and hidden,
but which God planned for us to understand before
time began. None of the rulers of this world have
understood this, for if they had, they would not have
crucified the Lord of glory. These are the things God
has revealed to us through the Spirit. We need to be
spiritual people in order to understand these things.
People who are unspiritual won't get it. But we have
the mind of Christ. (6-8)

YOU ARE SUCH BABIES!

But I admit, brothers and sisters, that I could not speak
to you as spiritual people, but as unspiritual, as babies
in Christ. I fed you with milk, not solid food, for you
couldn't take solid food. Even now you are still not
ready, for you are still living in the old, merely human
way. For as long as there is jealousy and quarreling
among you, doesn't that mean you are still living in the
old, unspiritual way and behaving according to merely
human inclinations? For when someone says, "I belong
to Paul," and another, "I belong to Apollos," aren't
you being merely human? (3:1-4)

RESPONDING TO PAUL'S LETTER AS A HOUSE CHURCH

Those of Apollos—Paul mostly has you in mind as he
attacks the "wisdom of the world." He speaks sarcastically toward those of you who value present-day wisdom
and learning and common sense. Be vigorous in defending
yourselves. Complain that it's not all black and white, as
Paul says it is. There is considerable overlap between the
wisdom Jesus taught and the best wisdom of the world.

How do you feel when Paul calls you "babies in
Christ," able only to take milk? Isn't that demeaning? Is
Paul talking only to you who belong to Apollos, or to the
other factions as well? Isn't conflict a two-way street?

Those of Paul—While Paul seems at first to be critical of
all factions, you maintain that he lays the blame mostly
at the feet of the Apollonians. Support Paul against

any defense they make. Argue that you understand the "foolishness" of God through God's resurrection of the shamed and crucified Christ, thus upsetting all human assumptions of power and hierarchy and glory. Insist that their ways of pulling rank over the lower status believers is exactly what Paul calls the "human wisdom" which is doomed to destruction. Challenge their cozy connections to higher-ranking pagans in Corinth.

Those of Cephas—You agree with Paul's harsh condemnation of this present age and its doomed rulers. You believe that God's judgment is imminent. And you agree with Paul on the great reversal that the crucifixion and resurrection of Christ is bringing about. But you think Paul needs to say more about Jesus' life and teachings and the importance of Torah observance. Peter has told you about much diversity among the earliest communities of Jesus followers across the empire, such as between the churches in Jerusalem, Rome, and Alexandria, or those founded by Paul.

Those of Christ—You enthusiastically agree with Paul's upside-down theology. Once you were "nobodies" and now as God's children and members of God's vanguard assemblies, you are "somebodies." Show how you have experienced God's wisdom and how the new age under Christ has transformed your own lives. But if God has chosen the "foolish, weak, insignificant, and contemptible" of the world, what might this say about your enslaved status?

DEBRIEFING AND APPLYING

First discuss among yourselves what it was like for you to play your role in the simulation, responding to questions such as: When were you most able to identify with your character? When the least? When were you particularly uncomfortable? inspired? confused? angry?

Then raise some of the following questions about applying this passage for today:

1. Does our "present age" also reject God's purposes? To what extent are we part of a modern-day "empire" in which the rulers of our time pursue

status, power, fame, wealth, and conspicuous consumption at the expense of the common good? [3]

2. Does God today choose "nobodies" to shame the "somebodies"? Any examples?

3. Reflecting on these chapters, N. T. Wright urges, "Let us not settle for a gospel which allows the world's power games to proceed without challenge."[4] What evils do you think the church should be resisting that it is not?

4. How do you take Paul's message about God's upside-down values to congregations of comfortable middle or upper-middle classes, whose members benefit from the way things are?

5. Is the human wisdom of today so totally opposed to the wisdom of God, as Paul says of his day? What about scientific research, weather forecasting, psychotherapy, or self-help "wisdom"?

6. Does Paul come across as domineering or authoritarian in this passage? How has his passionate style helped or hurt in the life of the church?

---

3. Walter Wink terms this a domination system, the overarching reality that he describes in detail in *Engaging the Powers*.
4. Wright, *Paul for Everyone: 1 Corinthians*, 28.

10

FIELD HANDS AND MASTER BUILDERS
IMAGES OF UNITY

🮋🮋🮋🮋🮋🮋🮋🮋🮋🮋🮋🮋

1 CORINTHIANS 3:5–4:21

At the close of our last reading (3:4) Paul uses images of babies who need milk to puncture the "puffed-up" self-images of his listeners who think they are superior to the other believers. But this jab is not the end of Paul's first major point. Before Paul deals with specific problems in the Corinthian assemblies, he lays out his theological argument for the need for unity.

But this is not abstract theology. Paul is confronting a church that is dividing into factions tied to the personalities and egos of individual leaders. Some of you know from experience how destructive it can be when leaders become rivals and work against each other rather than for the common good.

Although four factions are dividing the churches (1 Corinthians 3:5–4:20), it appears that Paul sees "those of Apollos" as the major group challenging him. Remember that all the believers are recent converts from the past three or four years. Many still carry out the values and practices of the surrounding secular Roman culture of exploitation and status seeking.

Scale model of the Temple on the Temple Mount in Herodian Jerusalem, shortly before it was destroyed in 70 CE (Israel Museum, Jerusalem).

With such dissension and rivalry, now would be the time to call in some trained mediator from outside to call the factions together and work things out. But there is only Paul to intervene, and he is hardly a disinterested observer. Can Paul set aside his own interests and ego enough to lower the tensions and rivalries, rather than heighten them?

UNDERSTANDING THE BACKGROUND

Relation between Paul and Apollos. Paul insists that he is not competing with Apollos, nor does he essentially disagree with Apollos's teaching. Though different, their work has a common purpose. Perhaps Apollos's more Hellenistic education in Alexandria, a great center of Greek philosophy, and of the great Jewish philosopher Philo makes him sound more scholarly and cultured than Paul, but their aims are the same. In this way, Paul offers himself as an example for the Corinthians to imitate. He will not take the bait of competing against Apollos and thus increasing the conflict.

The church as temple. When Paul wrote this letter, the magnificent Herodian temple was still standing and represented to most Jews the holiest place in the world—the place where the very presence (*shekinah*) of Yahweh dwelt. Paul now claims that a small body of believers replaces the temple in Jerusalem—a radical claim indeed!

Since the discovery of the Dead Sea Scrolls, we have learned that another group of Jews, the Qumran community of Essenes living by the Dead Sea, was making a similar claim. This priestly, law-observant community saw itself as a temple-in-waiting until God would destroy the current corrupt temple system. But Paul's claim that both Jewish *and* Gentile Jesus-believers comprised God's temple is truly groundbreaking.

Paul's use of Scripture. When Paul says, "it is written," he is referring to the books of Job and Psalms in the Hebrew Scriptures, the Bible of the time. He does so to emphasize that *justice* is a major issue within the Corinthian assemblies. In the phrase "catching the wise in their own craftiness" (3:19, from Job 5:13), he is referring to those whose economic schemes abuse the needy, much like huge banks today have caused millions of home foreclosures and loss of retirement savings. When the wise are thus trapped, "injustice shuts its mouth" (Job 5:16). Paul's reference to Job here implies that, in the Corinthian situation, "the conflict over 'wisdom' has a socioeconomic dimension."[5]

Then in 3:20, Paul references Psalm 94, which calls upon the Lord to avenge those who "pour out their arrogant words," "crush your people" (v. 5), "kill the widow and the stranger," and "murder the orphan"(v. 6). Paul's paraphrase asserts, "The Lord knows the thoughts of the wise, that they are futile," thus heaping words of condemnation on the conduct of those who think they are "wise."[6]

"Nothing beyond what is written" (1 Corinthians 4:6). What does the above saying mean? It probably refers to the six Scriptures Paul has already quoted (in 1:19, 31; 2:9, 16; 3:19, 20), which are usually introduced by "it is written." Most have to do with issues of status and exploitation: wise and foolish, privileged and poor. This relates directly to 4:6c: "So that none of you will be puffed up, in favor of one against another."[7]

---

5. Hays, *1 Corinthians*, 57.
6. Ibid., 60.
7. Ibid., 69.

"We have become a spectacle." In 4:9 Paul declares that he and other apostles have become a spectacle to the world. Paul alludes here to the common practice of victorious generals marching home with their troops. Behind them trudge their prisoners, held up as war trophies and then executed or sold into slavery. Though this spectacle takes place far away in Rome, Corinthians have their own spectator sport—watching gladiators and condemned criminals fight each other to the death in the arena. With an amphitheater right on the outskirts of Cornth, this allusion would not be lost on Paul's audience. Paul sees the puffed-up ones as the spectators, watching the spectacle of the apostles suffering and dying in the arena and thinking of themselves as superior.[8]

A "stick" or a "rod of correction"? In 4:14-21, Paul's tone changes to that of a loving father who wants to correct and discipline his children. The "stick" (NRSV) or the "whip" (NIV) of verse 21 is better translated the "rod of correction." Proverbs 22:15 and 23:13-14 encourage fathers to use such a rod to "drive away folly" from their children.[9]

PREPARING FOR THE SIMULATION

Those of Apollos—You might want to argue that there is a difference between what Apollos teaches compared to what Paul teaches. Those of Paul challenge this on the basis of Paul's words. You could retort that you heard with your own ears what Apollos taught about the need for intellectual and spiritual attainment. You would hear Paul's statements criticizing arrogance as intended for you and would resent them, especially his comment about needing to come and spank you "with a rod of correction" (v. 21).

Those of Christ—You might wonder why Paul sees the role of apostles as a miserable "spectacle to the whole

---

8. Noted by Balch in a presentation on "Two Roman Colonies: Pompeii and Corinth" at the 2010 Annual Meeting of the Society of Biblical Literature. Think also of the recent series *The Hunger Games*, which depicts a future dystopian society doing the same thing—a reflection on our culture's present fascination with violent movies and video games.
9. Hays, *1 Corinthians*, 73.

world"—weak, hungry, and homeless (4:9-13). As prostitutes, abused and discarded women, you think you know better what it's like to be "the rubbish of the world" (v. 13).

Those of Paul—What might you think of his efforts to commend Apollos? Do you think the Apollonians have misunderstood Apollos and are using him against the other factions? Do you think Paul is betraying your faction by identifying with Apollos? Do you pick up any hints that Paul might distrust Apollos at some level?

Those of Cephas—Whose side are you on here? As Jews with precarious status in the Roman Empire, can you identify with Paul's description of apostles? Can you mediate between "those of Paul" and "those of Apollos"?

Phoebe or another reader performs 1 Corinthians 3:5–4:21:

CHURCH PLANTING AS FARMING

Who then, do you think, is Apollos? Who is Paul?
We're just servants through whom you came to
believe. I planted, Apollos watered, but God made the
crop grow. Neither of us is anything; only God gives
growth. Both planter and waterer work together, and
both of us will be paid wages according to our labor.
We are God's servants, working together. You—all of
you—are God's field! (3:5-9)

CHURCH BUILDING AS ARCHITECTURE

You are also God's building. I laid the foundation like
a skilled master builder, but others are building on it.
Be careful how you build! Of course there is no other
foundation than that of Jesus Christ—but at the com-
ing of the Lord, everyone's materials and workman-
ship will be exposed. Fire will test whether you have
built with gold, silver, precious stones, wood, hay, or
straw. If your work burns up, you may be rescued
only by the skin of your teeth! (10-15)

Church as temple

Don't you know that all you together make up God's
temple, and that God's Spirit dwells in you? If any
of you destroys that temple by your factions and
arguments, God will destroy you! For God's temple is
holy, and you all are that temple. (16-17)

Don't deceive yourselves and think that you are wise.
Worldly wisdom is foolishness with God, just as it
is written in Job 5:13 and Psalm 94:11—God will
ultimately outsmart those who rip off the poor. Don't
brag about any specific human leaders. Everything is
yours—Paul, Apollos, Peter, the world, life, death, the
present, or the future—all belong to all of you. And you
belong to the Messiah, and he belongs to God. (18-23)

Think of us, your leaders, as servants of Christ and
stewards of God's mysteries. It is only at the final
Judgment that the Lord will bring to light all hidden
attitudes and motivations and behaviors. Each one
will receive their own commendation. So do not
pronounce judgment before the Lord comes. (4:1-5)

I've used Apollos and myself as an example, so that
you may learn through us the meaning of the saying,
"Do not go beyond that which stands written." We
stick to these Scriptures against boasting, so that none
of you will be puffed up in favor of one over another.
What do you have that you did not receive? And if
you received it as a gift, why brag about it? (6-7)

Honorable Corinthians versus dishonored apostles

Indeed, you are acting as if you are kings—just like
the Stoics and Cynics! I rather wish you had become
kings, so that Apollos and I could be kings with you!
Instead, I think God has put us apostles at the end of
the victory procession, as though we were prisoners
sentenced to death. We have become a spectacle to the
whole world. (8-9)

*We are fools for Christ—but you are wise! We are
weak, but you are strong. You are honored, but we
are shamed. At this very hour we are hungry and
thirsty, dressed in torn clothes, knocked around and
homeless, tired from manual labor. When insulted,
we bless; when harassed, we put up with it; when
our good name is attacked, we speak kindly. We have
become like the scum of the earth, the grunge and
grime of all things, to this very day! (10-13)*

PAUL SCOLDS HIS CHILDREN

*Okay, so I was being sarcastic. But I don't want to
shame you. I'm just scolding you as my beloved children. You may have ten thousand tutors[10] in Christ,
but you do not have many fathers. But I became your
father through the gospel. So, as any good father
would, I want you to imitate me. For this reason, I
will be sending Timothy to you. He is my beloved and
faithful child, and he will remind you of my ways in
Christ Jesus. I teach the same things everywhere and
in every church.*

*Some of you, thinking I'm not coming back, have
become arrogant. But I will come back to you soon,
if the Lord wills, and I will find out not only what
these arrogant people say, but what they do! For the
kingdom of God does not depend on talk, but on
action. What would you prefer? Shall I come to you
with a rod of correction—or with love in a spirit of
gentleness? It's your call! (14-21)*

RESPONDING TO PAUL'S LETTER AS A HOUSE CHURCH

1. Which people in your house church best fit the
   description of those promoting factions?

---

10. The Greek word is *paidagōgos*, which is an attendant, usually a
slave, whose duty it was to conduct the boy or youth to and from
school and to generally supervise his conduct. Bauer, *A Greek-English
Lexicon of the New Testament*, 603.

2. In 3:5-15, how do each of you react to the idea that you (plural) are a field or a building? With what materials has your house church been built—with precious stones, straw, or what? If you are Jewish, do you like your house church being called a "temple" (3:16-17)?
3. Is judging wrong? (4:3-5). Don't higher-status people need to evaluate those below them who work for them? In the house church, what happens if lower-class people evaluate those above them?
4. Some of you patrons want to financially support Paul as your "house-philosopher." How do you react to Paul's description of apostles as the "rubbish of the world" (4:9-13)?
5. Since none of you have ever met Jesus, is it appropriate for Paul to ask you to imitate him? Do you see Paul as your father in Christ?

DEBRIEFING AND APPLYING

1. First evaluate your simulation. How well did you argue for or against Paul's teaching? What questions do you want to ask now?
2. In your experience of church, are some people "puffed up" and arrogant (4:6)? Regarding unity, how would Paul evaluate your congregation or denomination if he were here today? Are there factions that oppose each other?
3. The image of a building in 3:12-15 is provocative. What is the relationship between the foundation and the building materials? What does Paul mean by, "The builder will be saved, but only as through fire"?
4. Given Paul's concern about economic justice (4:16-23), how should churches deal with the growing economic inequality in America and elsewhere? Is it appropriate to talk about money and money management in church?

11

SCANDAL, LAWSUITS, AND SOLIDARITY

1 CORINTHIANS 5 AND 6

All too frequently, churches and denominations have been rocked to the core by revelations of scandalous sexual behavior among church leaders of all stripes. Sadly, this is nothing new. Around the year 54 CE, Chloe's people informed Paul not only about divisions among the faithful in Corinth, but also of a sex scandal involving one of the prominent believers. Imagine! A believer in Corinth is living with his stepmother![1] Paul is irate that the vanguard community he founded is allowing this to happen. "It is of a kind that is not found even among pagans," and they are "arrogant" about it! Why haven't the Corinthians removed the perpetrator of sexual scandal from among them (5:1-2)? Let's take a closer look.

UNDERSTANDING THE BACKGROUND

What exactly is the sexual offense? There are at least two options for how we might imagine this situation. Option 1: Andronicus, as we call him, is a young but prominent

---

1. Literally, the text reads, "someone has the wife of his father." Most translations use the term *have*, which in this context means a sexual relationship. The New American Bible and the NRSV say the man was "living with" his father's wife.

member of Chloe's people, one of the Apollonians who are better off. He generously uses his financial means and influence to help others. His mother died a while back, and so, as was common, his father remarried, this time to a much younger woman, Lydia, who is about the same age as Andronicus. Then Andronicus's father dies, leaving Lydia a widow. Andronicus develops a sexual relationship with his young stepmother, who is not one of the believers, perhaps to keep the inheritance in his family. Lydia could legally take her dowry with her if she married into another family.[2] This may explain why Paul links immorality with greed in 5:10-11.

Option 2, our view, is that the father is still living.[3] But if so, why does he tolerate being cheated by both his wife and his son? A possible explanation is that prosecution would have resulted in public humiliation for the father and in exile for both his son and wife, again with serious economic consequences.[4] And why does the Jesus-community tolerate such outrageous behavior? Money may also be the issue here, if Andronicus is one of the wealthier members and serves as a patron to the church.

Paul is also concerned because this behavior violates Hebrew law. "Cursed be anyone who lies with his father's wife," says Deuteronomy 27:20 (echoed in Leviticus 18:8 and 20:11). Paul's outrage implies that he sees his Gentile converts belonging to Israel's covenant community, and thus subject to the same moral restrictions as were Jews.[5]

But what does Paul mean when he says that "this is of a kind [of incest] not found even among pagans" (5:1)? According to Bruce Winter, Roman law was far more strict about adultery and incest when the woman involved was legally married.[6] If Andronicus's father had died, his stepmother would no longer be married. Such adultery/

2. Chow, *Patronage and Power*, 82ff.

3. The Greek of 5:1c uses the infinitive "to have" in the present tense— in that the woman is still the wife of the father. Winter, *After Paul Left Corinth*, 48.

4. Ibid., 49–52. Winter discuss additional legal complexities related to this issue.

5. Hays, *1 Corinthians*, 80.

6. Winter, *After Paul Left Corinth*, 48.

incest was not prosecuted. Since most men married wives at least ten years younger than themselves, Andronicus's behavior must not have been uncommon in the Roman context.

One last puzzle: why is Paul so much more incensed by Andronicus's behavior than that of men who visit prostitutes in 6:12-20? This is probably because the first transgression is also against Roman law, whereas the second is not. Paul does not want his churches to get in trouble with the state for reasons he does not approve of in the first place.

What is "destruction of the flesh"? Paul asks the Corinthians to "hand over this man to Satan for the destruction of the flesh" (5:5). Perhaps Paul's demand is so harsh because he had previously written the Corinthians not to associate with sexually immoral or greedy believers (5:9). But this hardly means killing the sinner. "Flesh" for Paul means the spiritual state of being oriented away from God; its opposite is "spirit," being oriented toward God. The rest of the sentence then makes sense. Exclude Andronicus from the fellowship of believers and leave him under the dominion of Satan. Hopefully he will repent "so that his spirit may be saved" (5:5), and he one day can rejoin the church.

In the honor-shame atmosphere of the Greco-Roman world, men were rarely shamed by their sexual practices, whereas for a woman, anything other than chaste, legitimate marriage was shameful—including single celibacy.[7] But in his response to Andronicus's behavior, Paul redraws the lines of honor and shame. In the Jesus-community, immoral male sexual behavior can be shamed, and unmarried women can bring honor to the single state (7:8).[8]

Christian freedom for men: are there no limits? In 6:12-20, Paul challenges the common cultural behavior of males and

---

7. This issue will arise in the next chapter. In this culture, marriage is the norm for everyone. A woman remaining single brings shame on her family.

8. Witherington, *Conflict and Community in Corinth*, 155.

tells them not to have sex with prostitutes! This discussion is set in the context of ethical guidelines that Corinthian men use. In verse 13 they argue, "Food is meant for the stomach, and the stomach for food," implying that, in the same way, sex is for the body and the body is for sex.[9] Paul likely has in mind elite banquets, which involve excessive eating, drinking and, in modern parlance, "hooking-up."

Chiseled into the sidewalk on the main street of Ephesus is a footprint pointing to the brothel established near the famous library. Upper-class males with leisure to read also have leisure for pleasure!

Gluttony and drunkenness were an accepted part of social life in Corinth, as were the promiscuous "after-dinners." For grand dinners such as the series of banquets given by the president of the Isthmian Games for the elite of Corinth, traveling brothels could be brought in by the host to cater for guests after the dinner.[10]

This is a class issue, since only elite men would be invited to such banquets. Paul sees this behavior as not only addictive (6:12) but destructive to the cohesion of the community which has been rescued from the realm of Caesar and baptized into the kingdom of God (6:11). Some of the prostitutes sent to those banquets could even be male and female slaves from the house churches! [11]

---

9. Wright, *Paul for Everyone: 1 Corinthians*, 72. It is common for men to view "using" food and sex in a similar way. Fredrickson, "Natural and Unnatural Use in Romans 1:24-27: Paul and the Philosophic Critique of Eros," 197–222.

10. Winter, *After Paul Left Corinth*, 88.

11. The words translated in v. 9 as "male prostitutes" (*malakoi*) and "sodomites" (*arsenokoitai*) in the NRSV have been much discussed by scholars. *Malakoi* literally means "the soft ones," and *arsenokoitai* is so rare no one can be completely sure of its range of meanings. For Paul to condemn all male prostitutes is problematic, since many were slaves who were victims, not perpetrators, and had no choice but to submit.

One thing is clear: As a Jew, Paul knew nothing of consensual love relationships between persons of the same gender. It was assumed people were "bisexual", and all same-gender sexual relations appear to have been exploitative, whether in the form of male prostitution, a master's forced sex with his slaves, or an older man of privilege having his way with his adolescent "boy-toy." For additional insights, see

Here are remains of the *bema*, or "place of judgment" in the Forum. Paul knew this place, having himself been arrested and judged here by Gallio, governor of Achaia in 50 CE (Acts 18:12-17). Is this the place where Jesus-followers were suing each other?

The problem with lawsuits in a domination system. Paul has also heard about believers suing each other in those impressive Roman courts in downtown Corinth. This is another example of class inequality and exploitation. The scales of Roman justice are not blind, and they greatly favor the "somebodies" over the "nobodies." Bribery is rife, and who can pay except the wealthy? Persons of lower rank are not allowed to marry a person of higher rank.[12] Court proceedings are notorious for unbridled language, defamation of

---

the essays by Robert Jewett and David Frederickson in *Homosexuality, Science, and the "Plain Sense" of Scripture*, ed. Balch.

We suggest reserving this discussion for another time when it can receive the in-depth consideration it deserves. Focusing only on the terms above can pull a group discussion away from Paul's main criticism of elite men using their status and wealth to dominate others in the church sexually and in Roman law courts. Resources to help the church discuss this issue include *Congregations Talking about Homosexuality*, ed. Beth Ann Gaede and Lull, *1 Corinthians*, 54–61.

12. Winter, *After Paul Left Corinth*, 60. "Lawsuits were conducted between social equals who were from the powerful of the city, or by a plaintiff of superior status and power against an inferior."

character, public shaming, and bitter wrangling.[13] The present strife in the house churches must be spilling over into pagan law courts and further splitting the community apart. Work out your disagreements within the Jesus-community, and don't sue each other at all, says Paul (6:4-8).

Preparing for the Simulation

Take a few minutes with your faction to clarify your social status and how each of these issues might affect you as elite, slave, or lower class, as female or male, as observant Jew or former pagan Gentile. How do you react to the principle "all things are lawful," which some of your house church members promote?

Reader performs 1 Corinthians 5:1–6:20:

Deal with the Sex Scandal!

It is actually reported that there is sexual immorality among you—a kind that is not found even among pagans: a man has his father's wife! And you are arrogant about it! Instead you should be filled with grief. You should have expelled this man.

Even though I'm not with you, I am present in spirit. I have already pronounced judgment on the man who has done such a thing. When you are assembled together in the name of the Lord Jesus and I am there with you in spirit too, you must hand this man over to Satan for the destruction of the flesh, so that his spirit may be saved on the day of the Lord.

You shouldn't be boasting. Don't you know that a little yeast leavens the whole batch of dough? Clean out the old yeast so that you may be like a new batch of unleavened dough as for Passover. Live the new creation, the new life. For Christ, our paschal lamb, has already been sacrificed. Therefore, let us celebrate our Passover feast, not with the yeast of the old life,

---

13. Ibid., 58–67.

*the life of depravity and evil, but with the unleavened
bread of the new life of sincerity and truth. (5:1-8)*

WATCH WHOM YOU ASSOCIATE WITH

*I wrote to you in my previous letter not to associate with
sexually immoral persons. I did not mean you should
have no dealings at all with immoral people of the world
at large, like greedy scammers or idol worshipers. To do
that, you'd have to withdraw from the world altogether.
What I mean is that you should not associate with any
sister or brother who is sexually immoral, or greedy,
or an idolater, slanderer, drunkard, or swindler. Do not
even eat with someone like that. It's not my business to
worry about people outside. Isn't it the people inside you
should worry about? God is the judge of those outside.
God's law in Deuteronomy says, "Drive out the wicked
person from among you." (5:9-13)*[14]

STAY OUT OF ROMAN COURTS

*How dare any of you take a grievance against one
of your fellow believers before Corinth's corrupt and
unjust law courts instead of before God's people?
Don't you know God's people will judge the world?
So why aren't you competent to judge smaller
matters? Why are you going to judges for whom the
church has no respect at all? You should be ashamed!
Isn't there anyone among you wise enough to be
your judge? Then you wouldn't have to sue a fellow
believer—and before corrupt unbelievers at that!*

*Actually, it's already a horrible setback to have any
lawsuits at all against each other. Wouldn't it be better
just to accept mistreatment or loss? To think that you
are wronging and defrauding fellow believers!*

*You know that people who do wrong will not share
in God's kingdom. Don't be fooled. Neither immoral*

---

14. Deuteronomy 13:5; 17:7.

*people of inappropriate sexual behavior, nor idol
worshipers, nor adulterers, nor thieves or the greedy,
nor drunkards or slanderers, nor scammers will
inherit the kingdom of God. Some of you used to be
among these, but you were washed clean, you were
made holy, you were made right with God through
the name of the Lord Jesus, the Messiah, and in the
Spirit of our God. (6:1-11)*

Your body is a temple

*"All things are lawful for me," you say—but remem-
ber, not all things are helpful. I might say, "All things
are lawful for me"—but I'm not going to let anything
control me. "Food is meant for the stomach and the
stomach for food," you insist. Yes, and God will eventually destroy both. The body, though, is not meant
for immorality, but for immortality. The body is meant
for the Lord, and the Lord for the body. God raised
the Lord Jesus, and God's power will raise us too.*

*Don't you know your bodies are members making
up the body of Christ? Can one take parts of Christ's
body and join them to a prostitute? Never! Don't you
know that one who joins himself with a prostitute
becomes one body with her? Scripture says: "The two
shall become one flesh."*[15]

*Keep away from immorality! Most sins occur outside
the body; but immorality involves sinning against
your own body. Your body, you know, is a temple
of the Holy Spirit that God gave you, so you are not
your own property. You were bought at a high price,
so use your body for the glory of God. (12-20)*

Responding to Paul's letter as a house church

1. Regarding the incest of Andronicus, do you
   agree with Paul's drastic judgment? What does

---

15. Genesis 2:24.

your faction have to gain or lose in terms of
prestige, social connections, wealth, or moral
integrity if the community decides to put him out
of their fellowship?

2. What response do you slaves—who have no
control over your own bodies—make to Paul?
On the other hand, what grievances might you
bring to the house church for judgment?

3. Have you won cases in the law courts against
someone of lower status? Were any of you
poorer persons caught and prosecuted for steal-
ing food?

4. Apollonians, could you bring a grievance to be
settled in your house church if some of those
judges in 6:1-6 were your clients or slaves?

DEBRIEFING AND APPLYING

1. How did each of you feel this time in acting out
your role? Different from last time?

2. What is church discipline like in your denomination or congregation? Is it different for church
leaders and laity? Would you use this passage as
a basis for church discipline today?

3. Compare the Roman law courts with our North
American justice systems today. Do social class
and wealth still make a difference?

4. Is it ever morally appropriate for a Christian or
congregation or denomination to sue? How do
we remain faithful to Paul's concern about working out issues in nonexploitative ways?

5. The refrain "all things are permissible for me"
has a contemporary ring. How is individualism a
problem in church and society today? Might the
church's moral stance regarding sexual expression be changing?

6. Discuss the issue of boundaries. How can we be
faithful to the values of Jesus' kingdom while
living in our global empire of capitalism and
militarism? How can church members support
each other?

12

SLAVERY, SEX, AND FAMILY
DOES PAUL POINT BEYOND
DOMINATION?

1 Corinthians 7

"Our wedding is a week after graduation." Many young people in Christian colleges or socially conservative churches feel a strong pressure to get married. Jokes abound about young women going to college to get an MRS degree rather than a bachelor's degree. Leaders in these churches preach, and parents encourage, sexual abstinence before marriage—hence, the rush to tie the knot.

However, a recent survey of marriage practices in the United States highlights very different trends. Not only is the average age at marriage moving upwards, but close to half the children born in 2008 were born to unmarried parents, especially among those with a high school education or less.[1] The report asks whether marriage itself is becoming a privilege primarily for the educated and elite classes. If social roles and sexual practices in Western societies have shifted significantly within even one generation, we can be sure the meanings of marriage and family have

---

1. Luscombe, "Who Needs Marriage? A Changing Institution." Forty-one percent, to be exact, and eight times the percentage fifty years earlier. *Time*, www.time.com/time/nation/article/0,8599,2031962-4,00.html.

changed and evolved much in the twenty centuries since Paul discussed these issues in his letter to Corinth.

Although topics relating to sexuality carry over from 1 Corinthians 6, we now begin a new section of this letter. Paul first deals with the *oral* report from Chloe's people (1:10–6:20), then begins responding to the *written* letter others have sent. Chapter 7 opens with four Greek words that mean, "now concerning the things about which you wrote . . . " The phrase, "now concerning . . ." will be repeated in 7:25; 8:1; and 12:1. Believers in Corinth have specific questions about how to live as God's people in a pagan culture. They hope Paul can advise them.

Sadly, we no longer have their letter. For example, in 7:1, where Paul writes, "It is well for a man not to touch a woman," it is important to know that Paul did *not* believe that statement but is quoting from their letter![2]

What follows are Paul's own reflections about marriage, sexual relations, virginity, celibacy, widows, and the related plight of slaves. Sometimes he uses "the Lord's" authority, other times he states his own opinion. He encourages people to stay in the condition in which they were when first called into the body of Christ (7:17), but he allows for some exceptions.

UNDERSTANDING THE BACKGROUND

How important is the body? How can it be that some men are visiting prostitutes (6:12-20) and apparently others say that a man should not touch a woman? No wonder they don't get along! Yet both attitudes ride on the same assumption: spirit is superior to physical matter, and thus the body is not important.[3]

We can call these different attitudes about the body "libertine" and "ascetic." The Libertines say, "Since the body isn't important, why worry about how we use it? You can't enjoy food and sex forever! Let's have a good

---

2. The New International Version (NIV) implies that this is Paul's statement by translating, "It is good for a man not to marry." But the literal Greek word is "to touch," which is a euphemism for sexual intercourse. It cannot be limited to marriage, since Paul has just discussed men seeking out prostitutes for sex (6:12-20).

3. Barr, *New Testament Story*, 128–32.

time while we still can!" On the other hand, the Ascetics say, "OK, the body isn't important, but it gets in the way of our spiritual lives. So if it feels good, it's wrong. Deny fleshly desires. Eat only enough to survive—and no sex!" This may explain the wildly opposing attitudes between chapters 5–6 and 7:1.

Marriage and family life in the Roman Empire. Modern Western ideals of marriage assume people marry because, besides common interests, they are in love. In contrast, marriages in this culture are arranged by families mainly on the basis of economics and class status. Among the elite, passing on wealth and maintaining public honor are all-important. For them marriage is an unequal, patriarchal arrangement, with the husband having greater power and authority and usually being around ten years older than his wife. Such arrangements are more like uncle and niece, so that peace, economic security, and lack of conflict in the family are higher ideals than equality and companionship.[4]

Whether because of arranged marriages, lack of privacy, or daily drudgery centered in the household, people in Rome's empire look beyond the family for pleasure and entertainment. After bearing several children (if at least two are sons), wives may not want to risk another pregnancy and may refuse sex. Husbands would then expect to satisfy their sexual desires by using their slaves or prostitutes of either gender.

Countercultural gender equality in 7:2-5. Both the libertine position and the ascetic prohibition Paul cites in 7:1 are from the perspective of male domination. In contrast, Paul's solution for married couples is fully egalitarian. Exactly what is asked of the wife is also asked of the husband. It is common in this culture to assume that the wife's body belongs to the husband, but *not* the reverse. For example, in the first century CE, Plutarch delivered a speech called "Advice to the Bride and Groom." In it he expects the wife to be faithful to her new husband, but he

---

4. Witherington, *Conflict and Community in Corinth*, 170–71.

also tells her to accept her spouse's casual sexual encounters "with a maid-servant or with high-class prostitutes at dinners."[5] Paul, on the other hand, assumes faithful monogamy on the part of *both* partners.

A famine makes an impact. There is evidence that during the 40s and 50s of the first century, serious grain shortages caused much hunger in the region.[6] Famine always falls most heavily on the poor, so Paul is keenly aware of the "present distress." This may explain why married couples might decide against sexual relations for a period of time, since they cannot feed another child. Abortion and infanticide are the usual methods of contraception, but they are not moral options that are open to the early Jesus-followers. Nevertheless, Paul advocates self-restraint for married couples only for a short period of time, "so that Satan may not tempt you because of your lack of self-control" (7:5).

Paul's apocalyptic world view. However, for unmarried men and women, Paul advocates staying unmarried (vv. 25-35), not only because of the "present crisis" but also because "the present form of this world is passing away" (v. 31). God is about to intervene in human history, so this is no time for married persons to have divided loyalties between the Lord and their spouse (vv. 32-35). Note, however, that this is "no command of the Lord," just Paul's advice—for those who can control their bodily desires.

Pollution and purity. Some believers are wondering if they have to divorce or separate from their unbelieving

---

5. Plutarch, *Moralia 140B*, "Advice to the Bride and Groom." Referred to in Winter, *After Paul Left Corinth*, 124.

6. Because so many people live at subsistence level, even the fear of famine can lead to riots. Bruce Winter bases his argument on the fact that, during this time, one of Corinth's leading citizens, Tiberius Claudius Dinippus, appears to be given responsibility for relieving grain shortages. For this benefaction to the city, a set of inscriptions is erected in his honor, exceeding the honor of any other first-century patron in Corinth. Note that in the pre-Isthmian Games reception in appendix 1, the Corinthian *duoviri* announce that they are appointing Claudius Dinippus to again be grain master.

spouses. Here Paul also counters the conventional view of holiness. Rather than pagan contact spiritually polluting a believer, Paul insists it's the other way around. Holiness is more powerful and contagious, and spreads to both spouse and children.

Circumcision and competing in the nude. Because athletes perform nude in the games, young Jewish men who want to compete are often scorned because of their circumcision—considered a mutilation. So an operation called an *epispasm* can be performed to remove the evidence. Paul counsels against this, just as he does not require circumcision for Gentile men who join the Jesus Movement (v. 18).

Does Paul want slaves to be slaves? Verse 21, depending on its translation, sounds oppressive toward slaves. The Greek literally reads, "A slave were you called? Do not let it matter to you. But if indeed you are able to become free, rather use [it]." For this reason, over against the NRSV, we prefer the NIV here: "Were you a slave when you were called? Don't let it trouble you—although if you can gain your freedom, do so."[7]

Chapter 6 discusses Roman slavery in more detail, but note here that Paul's discussion of marriage, sex, singleness, and the body has huge implications for slaves in these house churches. Slaves cannot marry, nor are they "single," for their very bodies belong to someone else. Most of the time they are regarded simply as "bodies" without honor or personal dignity. They must be sexually available to their owner or, if they are used as a slave prostitute, to anyone who pays the owner. We might wish Paul to be clearer, but surely any Jew of this time—who celebrates Passover as liberation—would never condone slavery. Still, unpaid slaves are the engines of empire, and Paul has no power to change it.

---

7. The NRSV reads, "Were you a slave when called? Do not be concerned about it. Even if you can gain your freedom, make use of your present condition now more than ever." (But it adds a footnote: "avail yourself of the opportunity.") How we interpret this verse will affect our view of Paul on the issue of slavery. For an extended discussion, see Harrill, "Paul and Slavery," 575–607.

PREPARING FOR THE SIMULATION

The issues in this chapter not only reflect division among our four factions, but cut across lines of gender and of slave or free status. Clarify in your house church who is married, what were the marriage arrangements, and whether the spouse is a believer or not. Who are the libertines (all men?) and who are the ascetics? What attitudes will they take on the above issues? Who would like a divorce? Who prefers to remain single, and for what reason? How much do food shortages affect you?

Of you slaves in the house church, how many have owners who are not believers? What is your relationship to your master? Can we assume both Jewish and Gentile Christian slave owners will not sexually abuse their slaves? Ask the slaves themselves!

As you listen to Paul's letter, try to decide how counter-cultural, radical, or conservative he is. Where do you agree with him, and where would you challenge or disagree with him?

Reader performs 1 Corinthians 7:1-40:

PAUL'S OPINIONS ON MARRIAGE AND CELIBACY

Now concerning the matters you wrote about. You said, "It's good for a man not to touch a woman." But I say, because of temptation to immorality, every man should have his own wife and every woman her own husband. The husband should give his wife her conjugal rights, and likewise the wife to her husband. Both husband and wife have authority over each other's bodies. Don't deprive each other unless you want to set aside a short time just for prayer. Otherwise you may give in to temptation. (7:1-5)

Here's what I think: I wish everyone were single like myself. But I realize each has a particular gift from God, but not all gifts are the same. To the unmarried and widows, I say, remain unmarried as I am. But if you are not self-controlled, marry rather than burn with passion! (6-9)

To the married folks, the Lord—not I—has commanded that the wife should not separate from her husband. But if she does, she shall remain unmarried or else be reconciled to him. The husband also shall not divorce his wife. (10-11)

Jesus never dealt with the following problem, but here is my advice: if a brother or sister has a spouse who is not a believer but who agrees to stay married, the believer should not divorce her or his spouse. For the unbelieving spouse is actually made holy through this marriage. If not, your children would be unclean, but as it is, they are also holy. But if the unbelieving partner wants to separate, let it be so. You are not bound in that case. For God has called us to peace, and perhaps in either case you may be instrumental in saving your spouse. (12-16)

PAUL'S RULE IN A TOP-DOWN WORLD OF DOMINATION

In general, here is my rule in all the churches I have planted: accept the social situation in which you find yourself. If you were circumcised, don't try to remove the evidence. If you are not circumcised, don't seek it. It doesn't matter either way—only obey God's commandments. (17-20)

This is also true of slaves. Were you enslaved when God called you? Do not be worried about not being able to be sexually pure in your condition. If you can gain your freedom, do so! Even if you were a slave when called, you are free in Christ, just as believing free persons are slaves of Christ. Free persons should not sell themselves into slavery. Remain with God in whatever condition you are in presently. (21-24)

COUNTERCULTURAL FOR A REASON

Now concerning virgins, I don't know of any teaching from the Lord. But I think, in view of the present distress, you should also remain as you are. If married, don't seek to separate. If not married, stay that way. But you don't sin if you do marry. Yet those who marry will experience physical hardship, and I would spare you that. (25-28)

*What I mean is that we're running out of time. Let
those who have spouses live as though they had none.
In all you do, live as though you already have one
foot in the age to come. (29-31a)*

*Indeed, the present form of this world is passing
away, and I want you to be free from worries.
Married people worry about making a living and
pleasing their spouse, but the single person can better
focus on the affairs of the Lord. I'm not saying this to
restrain you, but only to promote unhindered devotion to the Lord. (31b-35)*

*However, if a single man is behaving improperly
toward his fiancée, let them marry. That's not a sin!
But if a man can maintain a celibate relationship with
his virgin fiancée, let them remain unmarried. The
man who marries does well—but the one who can
remain single does even better! (36-38)*

*The same is true for a widow. She can marry again
if she wishes. But I think she is more blessed if she
remains single. I know these are my opinions, but I
think I too have the Spirit of God! (39-40)*

Responding to Paul's letter as a house church

Since Paul has freely shared his own opinions, each person should freely share her or his own!

1. If you are a slave, is Paul encouraging you—or
   keeping you in your place? Are you being abused
   or treated with respect? If the gospel has freed you
   to speak out, what would ask of your owner?
2. As a married or engaged person, what do you say
   to Paul's recommendations about physical inti-
   macy? Wives, do you sense a breath of liberation?
3. As a widow or unmarried person, how do you
   react to Paul's admonitions to "stay as you are"?
4. How do you more powerful (male) members
   feel about Paul's admonitions about sexual
   behavior and, specifically, your behavior?

5. Paul's position on staying single is very countercultural. Are you in a social position to even consider this? What pressures come to bear on you to marry if you are single—or to arrange marriages for your children?
6. What is the impact of the famine and food shortages on you?

DEBRIEFING AND APPLYING

1. In your role in Corinth, what level of comfort or discomfort did you feel about Paul's discussion of marriage, singleness, and sex?
2. Do husbands still have more authority over their wives than vice versa? What would Paul say about that today?
3. In your role, what level of comfort or discomfort did you feel about Paul's discussion of slavery?
4. Historically, supporters of human slavery have used this chapter to justify it. How might a more progressive interpretation have affected the course of history?
5. How does the Corinthian sex-saturated culture compare with our culture today?
6. Even more people are enslaved in the world today than in Rome's empire. What is the church's responsibility?

13

EATING AT THE "TABLE OF DEMONS"?

1 CORINTHIANS 8 AND 10

I (George) once had a church friend whose devotion to a certain pro football team was so great that his own personal life reflected the fortunes of the team. When they won, he felt great and strong and useful; when they lost, his whole way of life turned sour. His attitude toward others was colored with negativity and he often not only felt sick but would actually become ill. For this friend, being a fan of this team had become a form of idolatry. He was making something that was limited into that which is ultimate. Football was affecting his best self, his friends, his family, and his work. Football had become god-like for him. It had become an idol.

Venerating stone images of a Caesar or a golden calf, or sacrificing animals to so-called divinities may seem quaint and foreign to our culture. But if worship means giving ultimate devotion to something, then the question of what or whom we worship is a very real issue for all times and places.

In chapters 8–10 Paul seeks to prevent the Corinthian believers from returning to idolatrous practices, to avoid the slippery slope that leads away from the shared life of the Jesus community. The dynamic of competing moral realms with opposing lures and invitations is like a force field.[1] We can choose to be in certain places, to do certain things, to expose ourselves to certain influences that either lead to a healthy moral climate, "the table of the Lord," or to an unhealthy one, "the table of demons" (10:21).

In this way Paul raises critical questions that are no less relevant today: can I participate in activities I do not believe in and not be affected by them? What if some members of the community have certain scruples or would experience real temptations because of what I do? What's the relation between the exercise of my rights and privileges and the welfare of others, especially the less privileged?

UNDERSTANDING THE BACKGROUND

The "slogan-and-answer" format. Like Paul's chapter on family and household relationships, this section also begins with "Now concerning . . . " This indicates another topic raised by the educated, influential members of the Corinthian house churches. This time the subject is food sacrificed to idols. Again, Paul begins his answer quoting a slogan from the Apollos faction: "all of us possess knowledge." Again Paul replies, "Knowledge puffs up, but love builds up." Ouch!

These pithy sayings, these Corinthian aphorisms, are akin to phrases we might use today, like "might makes right," "I love my country right or wrong," or "better to have loved and lost than not to have loved at all." In chapters 8 and 10 we find many of these slogans, including "all things are lawful" (10:2; see 6:12). Watch for this slogan-and-answer format[2] to discover the differences between Paul and those "belonging to Apollos."

"Many gods and many lords": the gods on the offensive. By the middle of the first century CE, one could speak of the gods being on the offensive. As we have noted, Emperor Augustus was grateful to the god Apollo for his history-changing victory over Mark Antony. Seeing the value of ritual as spiritual cement to unify his sprawling

1. Lull, *1 Corinthians*, 88.
2. Wright, *Paul for Everyone: 1 Corinthians*, 137.

empire, he instigated a religious revival. By the time of Paul's ministry, the city teemed with shrines, altars for public sacrifices, temples, statues of the gods and first family, and sacred inscriptions.[3] Paul has firsthand knowledge of Corinth's "many gods and many lords" (8:5) and the mighty moral force field they create.

Into this already supercharged environment of imperial religion comes the announcement that Corinth will host a special edition of the Isthmian Games to honor the emperor and imperial family. This is a great honor for the city and its leaders (see appendix 1 on the elaborate pregames reception). It further heightens the pressure on the Christian citizens to participate in these patriotic-religious festivities and ceremonies. Joining in is part of being a respectable citizen, and not joining can arouse suspicion. Besides, there might be some free meat and drink, plus some relief from the drudgery of the everyday grind.

The Corinthians are attracted to this civil religion because it connects them with the empire, with something larger than themselves. For lives that are often brutish and short, it identifies them with what was considered the entire civilized world. The great military victories of past and present are lifted up as their victories as well. Though they may have heard gruesome stories of Roman conquest, now they are being persuaded to identify with the conqueror.

At the same time some find comfort in a mystery religion. A woman might believe she is healed at a shrine of Asclepius and leave an offering of a terra cotta votive in the shape of the healed body part. Because they were shrouded in secrecy, little is known about the mystical rites of these religions. (See chapter 7 for other religious options.)

The problem of divided loyalties. One can begin to see why Paul is so adamant in warning against idolatry—the worship of any god or object other than the God of Israel and the Lord Jesus. First, such idol worship provides

---

3. For a thorough discussion of the overwhelming impact of the visual environment in the Roman Empire, see Zanker, *The Power of Images in the Age of Augustus.*

the spiritual cement holding together the entire system of domination under Rome. This structure sends scarce resources upward from the bottom to the top, from slaves and sharecroppers all the way up to the imperial family.

Second, the general moral ethos of imperial religion is, from the viewpoint of Jews like Paul, one of utter degradation. It is similar to the worship of idols condemned over and over again in Jewish Scriptures. Imperial religion is characterized by rampant self-gratification, sexual immorality, exclusion of all but the wealthy from full initiation, and grandstanding by the elite in their highly sought-after priestly posts. The legends of the gods are replete with cruelty, jealousy, sexual promiscuity, and murder, including infanticide, patricide, and matricide. And the behavior of the imperial families reflects in real time what happens in the legends about the gods.

Finally, Paul opposes "many gods and many lords" because he knows, from Israel's history and from his own experience in the empire, about the great temptation to "go along to get along" with the imperial religion and the domination system.

Eating idol meat: temple banquets versus private dinners.
Idol meat is the meat left after an animal is sacrificed to a god. Greeks and Romans believe that the gods only want to smell the smoke from the sacrificed animal, so only the fat and gristle are placed on the fire. The meat is then sold at the public market.

Temple banquets play a central role in the lives of the elite. A convenient and popular setting is the temple of Asclepius, where, in the reenactment in appendix 1, the reception for the Corinth elite was held. These banquets reinforce the ironclad hierarchical structures of life in the empire. They reaffirm each participant's acceptance of this ranking. The host seats participants according to their rank, sometimes offering better food to the higher-ups. For them, eating food sacrificed to the gods means literally taking in the god's being.

The dessert course may well be followed by music, dancing, and sexual enticements. The time together allows for networking; strengthening business, political, and per-

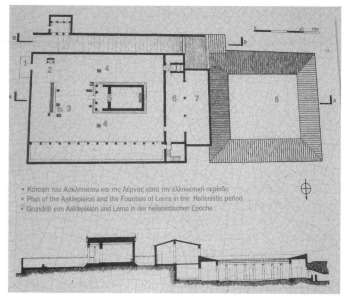

A floor plan and a side view of the Asclepieion, Corinth's healing center. The temple (5) and its altar (3) are enclosed and can accommodate large crowds of worshipers. The dining room and courtyard on the lower level are used for public meetings and private parties. The reception on the evening before the games was likely held here. Paul considers these banquets the "table of demons."

sonal ties; and reinforcing patronage relations: "If you do this for me, I'll do that for you." It is the traditional all-male smoke-filled room where things are *really* decided. For Paul, participating in these banquets is to sit down at the "table of demons" (10:21)—that is, the table of the domination system that God opposes. Yet, if you want to make it in Corinth, you need to respond to banquet invitations and to reciprocate by sponsoring your own.

In contrast, eating at a private dinner, even if idol meat is served, is not as serious for Paul if no one makes an issue of it (10:25-27). This is because "no idol in the world really exists" (8:4) and such a dinner doesn't necessarily partake in the same way in the elitist, social-climbing, anything-goes ethos of the domination system.

Is the demonic real? Paul places a stark choice before his readers: either sit at "the table of the Lord" or "the table of demons" (10:29). He suggests that there are demonic realms and force fields of life that actively resist the things of God. This demonic force has in principle been overwhelmed by God but is hanging around until the day of the Lord. Then, according to Paul, Christ will be ruler of all things. Tom Wright describes the demonic threat as "a matter of desires that well up from inside a person and reach out to objects and styles of life which reflect and copy forces, powers, and even divinities other than the one true God made known in Jesus the Messiah."[4]

Paul wants the new believers to protect each other from such temptation. Staying away from sacrificed food and temple banquets is especially important for those with a weaker moral consciousness and understanding (8:10-12).

Meat as a class issue. Eating meat means eating at the top of the food chain; meat is always the most expensive food. The vast majority of ancient people never ate meat except at special occasions like festivals when patrons might provide morsels for their clients.

Including Gentiles. Paul clearly believes non-Jews are included in "all Israel," since he refers to Israelites journeying in the wilderness as "*our* ancestors" (10:1-11). For him, a true Israelite is marked by faithfulness, not by pedigree.

PREPARING FOR THE SIMULATION

In the interest of time we will omit reading most of 1 Corinthians 9. We have discussed it in our sixth chapter on patronage when speaking about Paul's rejection of his right to receive financial support from patrons. Paul inserts this example from his own life to demonstrate the high cost of renouncing advantages and rights for the sake of others— exactly what he's asking of the more privileged members of the house church. If it would keep some sisters and brothers from stumbling, he will never eat meat (8:23). Neither should they—especially not at the "table of demons" (10:21).

---

4. Wright, *Paul for Everyone: 1 Corinthians*, 127.

Those of Apollos—Some of you can afford to buy meat in the market and are influential enough to be invited to banquets in a temple or home. You had written Paul assuming that eating sacrificed food and temple banqueting is acceptable because "idols really don't exist." You are surprised and shocked by Paul's response, and you want to defend the teachings you live by. You claim they are endorsed by Apollos and consistent with what you learned from Paul himself.

Those of Paul—You are eager to defend Paul. You think those sophisticated Apollonians don't take evil and temptation seriously enough and visit "the table of demons" whenever they are invited. Further, you emphasize the need for consideration of others—that love is more important than knowledge, and sometimes means rigorous self-denial.

Those of Cephas—You're with the Paulists. You especially like the recapitulation of Israel's history, with its serious warnings against idolatry—warnings you believe Gentiles don't always heed.

Those of Christ—As Gentiles you definitely fear being tempted back into idolatry. As it is, you dabble sometimes in goddess worship—after all, it's what helped you survive in previous days. You wonder about Paul's talk of renouncing things, but you see that he's really talking to the privileged Apollonians. He's not asking you as poor women to renounce what you don't have. If you are a slave pressed into after-dinner prostitution, you understand Paul's concerns very well!

Dionysia—You are excited by Paul's reference to athletes (9:24-27). This has been your life. He's speaking your language, and you really get it that discipline is necessary for the Christ-life. You vow to be careful about idolatry as you coach athletes.

The reader performs 1 Corinthians 8; 9:24-27; 10:1–11:1:

EATING IDOL-FOOD

Now concerning food sacrificed to idols: as you say, "we all possess knowledge." But knowledge puffs up, while love builds up. Anyone may claim to know something and still not have a full understanding. (8:1-3)

So when it comes to the eating of food consecrated to idols, we both know that "no idol in the world really exists," and that "there is no God but one." Indeed, even though there may be so-called gods in heaven or on earth, for us there is one God, the Father. Everything comes from him, and we belong to him. And there is just one Lord, Jesus Christ. Everything comes into existence through him, and we ourselves live because of him. (4-6)

Not everyone, however, knows this. Some still think of the food they eat as idol-meat because they were used for idol worship. This has given them a weak and damaged conscience. You say, "Food won't bring us close to God. We aren't worse off if we don't eat, and no better off if we do." All right, only take care that using this liberty of yours doesn't somehow become a danger to those with weak consciences and limited understanding. (7-9)

Let's say someone with a weak conscience sees you sitting down to eat in the temple of an idol. Since their conscience is weak, might they not be encouraged to eat food consecrated to idols? Then your "knowledge" causes utter disaster for the weak—your fellow believers for whom Christ died! If you thus sin against your brother or sister and wound their weak conscience, you are sinning against Christ. Instead, say, "If food is a cause of their downfall, I will never eat meat, for I will not be a cause of their downfall."(10-13)

COMPETE AS A WINNING ATHLETE

*Use self-discipline! I remind you that at the stadium
all the runners are competing for the prize, but only
one wins. In the same way you must run to win!
Athletes must engage in serious training and practice
self-control. They do this just to be crowned with a
wreath of dried celery leaves, but we run a race for
a crown that will never wither. So as I compete, I
don't run lackadaisically and I don't box as if I'm just
punching the air. Rather, I punish myself and discipline my body very rigorously. After exhorting others,
I don't want to be disqualified myself. (9:24-27)*

WARNINGS FROM ISRAEL'S HISTORY

*Remember, brothers and sisters, that our ancestors
were all baptized into the fellowship of Moses. They
passed safely through the Red Sea, and were guided
by a cloud in the desert. They all ate the same spiritual
food and drink. It came from the spiritual rock that
accompanied them, and that rock was our Messiah.
In spite of this, most of them failed to please God and
they were struck down in the desert. (10:1-5)*

*These things happened to warn us not to do what
they did. Don't become idolaters and worship false
gods like they did. The Bible says, "The people sat
down to eat and drink, and then they got up to amuse
themselves." We must not indulge in sexual immorality as some of them did, when 23,000 fell in a single
day. We must not grumble like some of them did, and
were destroyed by serpents. (6-10)*

*These things were written down as a lesson for us, for
whom the end of this age has come. So if you think
you are standing firm, watch out that you don't fall.
Every test that comes your way is normal for human
beings. God is faithful and will not let you be tested
beyond your strength. Along with any trial God will
also provide a way out and give the strength to endure
it. (11-13)*

Two kinds of tables

*Therefore, my dear friends, don't worship idols! I'm
speaking to you as intelligent people; weigh my words
carefully. The cup that we bless is a sharing in the life
and blood of Christ, isn't it? The bread that we break is
a sharing in the body of Christ, isn't it? The fact is that
we, as many as we are, share just one loaf that makes
us all one body. Consider the Jewish people of Israel.
Isn't there a fellowship among all those who eat the altar
sacrifice? What am I saying then? That food sacrificed to
idols is anything more than food, or that an idol is real?
No, not at all, but when unbelievers offer sacrifices, they
offer them to demons and not to God. I do not want
you to be table partners with demons. You cannot drink
the cup of the Lord and the cup of demons. You cannot
be a guest at the table of the Lord and at the table of
demons. Do you want to make Jesus angry? (14-22)*

In your freedom, consider others

*Again, you say, "All things are lawful"—but I say
that not all things are helpful. "All things are lawful,"
but not all things build you up. Do not seek your
own interests but the interests of others. You may eat
whatever is sold in the meat market without raising
any questions of conscience. After all, "the earth and
everything in it is the Lord's." If an unbeliever invites
you to dinner and you want to go, eat whatever is set
before you without raising any questions of conscience. However, if someone says to you, "This has
been offered in ritual sacrifice," then do not eat it. Be
considerate to the one who informed you, and for the
sake of his or her conscience. (23-30)*

*So whether you eat or drink, or whatever you do, do
everything for God's glory. Try not to offend Jews
or Greeks or the church of God, just as I try to be
helpful to everyone in everything I do, not seeking
my own interest, but the good of all, so that they
may be saved. Take me as your model, as I do Christ.
(10:31–11:1)*

Responding to Paul's letter as a house church

1. Is eating idol meat a big issue for you? Do those in your faction ever get meat to eat at all?
2. What does Paul mean by "strong" and "weak"? Which word describes you or your faction? Should the "strong" give up eating idol meat for the sake of the "weak"?
3. When are you tempted to return to your old ways and worship "many gods" and Caesars? Do you ever give in to this temptation?
4. Paul urges believers to stay totally away from temple banquets. Is this a problem for you and your faction? Would you forego these rights for church unity?
5. Paul says it's a choice between sitting at the "table of the Lord" and the "table of demons." Why can't you do both? Is there no neutral ground? What about the exception for private dinners with nonbelievers?

Debriefing and applying

1. Some suggest that the most tempting idols today are militarism, nationalism, self-gratification, materialism, and the indiscriminate right to own and carry guns. One writer says they promise much but deliver little of what they promise. What do you think?
2. What are contemporary examples of giving up freedom to protect the conscience of others more vulnerable? Alcohol? Modern media and technology? What else?
3. What might be some settings or situations, with their force fields, that are simply too dangerous to be around if you want to keep to your moral principles and your faith?
4. What metaphors other than athletics would you suggest for the training and discipline that Christians need today?

14

HAIRDOS AND HEADSHIP
THE CORINTHIAN WOMEN PROPHETS

▛▟▛▟▛▟▛▟▛▟▛▟▛

1 CORINTHIANS 11:2-16

This is one passage I (Reta) and the girlfriends I grew up with wished Paul had never written! In the Mennonite farming community in southeastern Pennsylvania where I was growing up in the 1950s, girls were expected to wear a white covering on their heads from the time we were baptized, usually around ages eleven or twelve. It was part of a long tradition with little stated justification—only that, if Paul said so, that's what we were supposed to do. Our high school math teacher told us it gave women equal authority with men (11:10) when we prayed or participated in church life.

The real issue, I think, was what Mennonites called "nonconformity to the world." Wearing a covering was an identity marker that set us apart from everyone else and, along with other clothing regulations, restricted women more than men in daily life. By the time I moved into a wider world as a young adult, I had long ago concluded this was an outdated cultural practice. And by then our denomination was moving away from the dress regulations of previous generations.

Ironically, as I came to know more evangelical and mainline Christians, I learned that they assumed this text taught female subordination—even though women in these churches did not wear a literal head covering. Conservatives thought women should submit, and liberals thought Paul was sexist!

What stands out for me (George) is the way the reference to women's subordination in this and other passages has been used to justify exclusion of women from pastoral leadership. In the 1960s the same Methodist church body that had so warmly welcomed me into the ordained ministry refused to ordain my soon-to-be spouse. This was despite our identical theological education and Tilda having demonstrated far greater skill in pastoral ministry than I—and despite the fact that Paul did not question women's leadership in worship, prayer, and prophecy. Operating out of a tradition of gender hierarchy and women's subordination, our bishop pounded his fist on the desk as he said to her, "I will never ordain another woman! I don't know what to do with the two I have [out of more than 500!]. . . . I consider women unappointable." What a painful time for her!

In many areas of church and society, the debate about gender roles continues. Can our simulation deepen our understanding of this challenging passage, which has been at the heart of this debate?

UNDERSTANDING THE BACKGROUND

Actually, we admit that we don't completely understand the background of this text—and we have a lot of company among prominent commentators! Richard Hays admits that "the line of argument is—by any standard—labored and convoluted."[1] David Lull remarks that this section "is perhaps the most obscure part of the letter."[2] Richard Horsley questions whether Paul wrote it at all: "In addition to its poor fit into the literary context, the vocabulary and content of the passage are strange for Paul."[3] Jouette

---

1. Hays, *1 Corinthians*, 183.
2. Lull, *1 Corinthians*, 96.
3. Horsley, *1 Corinthians*, 152.

Bassler asserts, "Paul probably wrote it, but his argument is inarticulate, incomprehensible, and inconsistent . . . One senses conflicting views within Paul shutting down the rational process, and where reason fails, emotion and tradition take over"[4]— this is especially evident in verse 16. We can, however, say a few things with some confidence:

The literary context. The setting of 1 Corinthians 11–14 is a worship service, the house church "assembly" (*ekklesia*) of believers, which probably takes place each evening or several times a week. Paul first (11:2-16) instructs men and women about what to wear or not wear to this occasion. Then he critiques the first part of the service, a full meal that includes the ritual of bread and cup (11:17-34). Worship, teaching, and study follow, during which some of the gifts of the Spirit, such as speaking in tongues and prophesying, are exercised. Here Paul again makes corrections and suggestions for improving the worship (chapters 12–14).

Trying to follow Paul's argument in 11:2-16. Here are some issues readers might logically raise about this text:

- Verse 2 must be ironic. Paul commends the Corinthian believers because they "maintain the traditions" he handed on to them. Really? Then why does he imply that some women (perhaps also some men) are *not* conforming to some traditions Paul thinks are important?

- Verse 3 lays out a distinct hierarchy of headship: God—Christ—man—woman. Egalitarian Christians today wince at what looks like a parallel to Imperial Roman hierarchy. Paul's consistent challenge to this inequality in the first ten chapters now seems to be overturned.

- How do we understand the Greek word *kephale* for "head"? Paul uses the term both metaphorically and literally (i.e., vv. 3-5). Is this just a clever way of arguing from metaphorical head-

---

4. Bassler, "First Corinthians and Community Disagreements," 32.

ship to a literal head that must somehow be
covered in women and uncovered in men? Or, as
some argue, does *kephale* mean "source," as in
the head or source of a river?

• In verses 7-9, Paul deliberately argues from a
patriarchal interpretation of the second creation
account in Genesis 2—that man reflects the
image of God, but woman reflects the image of
man, since the woman was created for the man
and not vice versa. In doing so, Paul disregards
Genesis 1:27, which says that male and female
were together created in the image of God.

• What do the angels in verse 10 have to do with
what women wear on their heads? Note also
that the text literally reads, "a woman ought to
have authority on her head." The NRSV adds "a
symbol of."

• By verse 11, Paul seems to reverse all he has said
about male priority. Here he writes that not only
"woman came from man," but also "man comes
through woman," while "all things come from
God"!

• When Paul says that "nature" teaches that for
men to wear long hair is degrading and that
women's long hair is their "glory" (11:13-15), he
seems to mean what we call "custom." *Nature*
grows men's and women's hair equally long,
while Greco-Roman *custom* dictates that men
have short hair and women have long hair.

• Paul concludes his argument in verse 16 rather
lamely: if anyone wants to argue, this is the
norm we have in all the churches. In other
words, this is such a settled issue that we're not
going to debate it!

• *One important note*: although Paul argues for
differences in appearance during worship, no

gender restrictions are placed on verbal participation and leadership.

Ancient views of gender. Dale Martin examines body issues at length.[5] Though we today assume two genders, ancient writers conceived of just one gender—with everyone on a wide continuum of maleness. Men are at the higher end of the spectrum, women at the lower end. *Man* is *the* representative of the human race. The female, said the philosopher Aristotle, is an imperfect male. Greeks and Romans agree that "not all males are masculine, potent, honorable, or hold power, and some women exceed some men in each of these categories. But the standard of the human body and its representations is the male body."[6]

Because women are a faulty version of male perfection, female flesh is more susceptible to pollution and disease. Spiritually and emotionally, women are seen as particularly subject to penetration and invasion by negative spiritual forces. They need protection on their heads. A woman's long hair is at the same time her honor and her shame, and must be covered in public.[7]

Hair or veils? While many translations understand the issue to be women wearing a veil in worship, the Greek text never refers to veiling as such, but to a woman's head being covered. Richard Hays, for example, believes women's covering is "to have the hair tied up on top of the head rather than hanging loose."[8] This makes sense of verse 15, which says women's long hair "is given to her for a covering." It is also a matter of shame. According to Hays, "For women to have loose hair in public . . . was conventionally seen as shameful, a sign associated either

---

5. Martin, *The Corinthian Body*, 230.
6. Laqueur, *Making Sex*, 62. Quoted in Martin, 230. Although this is beyond the scope of our present text, such thinking explains how Greco-Roman society was "bisexual." Young boys, effeminate men, and slaves [who had no honor] were also on the female end of the spectrum and thus could be penetrated, as were women.
7. Martin, *The Corinthian Body*, 236, 242–43.
8. Hays, *1 Corinthians*, 185.

with prostitutes or—perhaps worse from Paul's point of view—with women caught up in the ecstatic worship practices of the cults associated with Dionysius, Cybele, and Isis."[9]

Caesar Augustus in his role as high priest (*pontifex maximus*) of the Empire. Men veiled themselves to offer a sacrifice at a temple. Archaeological Museum at Ancient Corinth.

But most commentators believe these references imply wearing a veil or covering the head with one's toga. This appears to be the meaning in relation to men. "Roman males normally covered their heads for worship."[10] This statue of Augustus, now in the museum at ancient Corinth, portrays him as a veiled priest at a temple sacrifice. But Paul reminds men in verses 4 and 7 that it is shameful for them to pray with covered head. Why? Is he just being countercultural? There may be a clue in verse 3: "Christ is the head of every man." In other words, a man's first allegiance is not to his patron, his emperor, or any of the Roman gods, but to Christ alone. Therefore, do not worship with covered head as do those who worship other gods.

Women's lot—the consequences of subordination. Gender assumptions of female inferiority have real consequences for women in the Greco-Roman world. Antoinette Clark Wire notes that discrimination begins at birth. The standard form of birth control is to expose unwanted babies to the elements, perhaps on a trash heap. There they either die or are found and raised as slaves or prostitutes.[11]

9. Ibid.,185–86.
10. Crossan and Reed, *In Search of Paul*, 113.
11. Wire, *The Corinthian Women Prophets*, 38–39.

Almost all such rejected babies are girls, since sons carry on the family line, and daughters need wedding dowries to become part of someone else's family.

Unless they are from upper classes, most girls who do survive receive no formal education, but are trained to prepare food and manage a household. Married as teenagers, women are expected to bear children (on average they need to have five in order for at least two to survive). Childbirth itself is dangerous, and many women die. Because husbands are older, many women who survive are widowed. But they quickly remarry, both because of tradition and because widespread infanticide of girl babies results in a shortage of adult women.

The lot of Corinthian women, says Wire, is to be "under immediate threat of death at birth and again at childbirth, with prostitution or slavery for those who survived exposure, and early marriage without decision-making power in the family for the others."[12]

Who are those angels? In 11:10, Paul says women need authority on their heads "because of the angels." The most common interpretation is that it refers to Genesis 6:1-4, where "sons of God" [fallen angels?] improperly lusted after and took human wives.[13] This could then be an oblique reference to male believers allowing themselves to be distracted from worship by the sight of women's uncovered hair—but seen as the women's problem rather than the men's.

Yet another view is based on the root meaning of *angel* as "messenger" or "scout." The concern then is about observers looking in on the Jesus worshipers from the street and reporting unusual or "dishonorable" behavior that could cast suspicion on the vulnerable house churches.[14]

---

12. Ibid., 38–39. It is primarily women commentators who squarely place this passage in the context of the status and role of women.

13. Lull, *1 Corinthians*, 97.

14. Winter, *After Paul Left Corinth*, 133–38. "The vestibules of Roman houses were open to the street . . . Whether it was out of interest in the message or in order to report on what these unknown gatherings were all about, 'the meeting' (*ekklesia*) was open to all who wished to view its proceedings" (135).

Paul's "woman problem." We agree with Dale Martin that, as a person of his time, Paul simply did not think men and women were equal. Because of their physiology (as explained above), it was thought they could never attain the perfection of masculinity until the resurrection.[15] Paul's comment about women's subordination seems grounded in this worldview.

On the other hand, Paul knows about Jesus' ministry of radical inclusivity, shown in the way he risked scandal to embrace the poor, the sick, the foreigner—and to an extraordinary degree, women. Closer to home, in Paul's own experience in ministry he labors side by side with women coworkers. Junia is the only person he calls an "apostle" besides himself, her husband Andronicus, and the original twelve (Romans 16:7). He commends many women in his letters for their leadership in the churches, including Prisca, who worked alongside him in establishing the original community of believers in Corinth. In his greetings in Romans 16, he praises women leaders even more than the men.

In the Corinthian house churches to which he is writing, women share leadership in worship, praying and prophesying openly (11:4). Therefore in our simulation, Phoebe is Paul's benefactor and the *diakonos* (minister) of a house church in the nearby port city of Cenchreae (Romans 16:1-2), while Chloe heads the congregation we are role-playing. Out of his practical experience, Paul testifies to the interdependence of women and men (i.e., 1 Corinthians 7:1-5). And it is Paul himself who declared near the beginning of this letter that "God chose what is weak in the world to shame the strong" (1:26). Perhaps Paul is still a "work in progress"—but headed in the right direction!

PREPARING FOR THE SIMULATION

Those of Christ—You are the charismatic women prophets who know you have been transformed in Christ. You know that Paul himself says that "in Christ there is neither male nor female." You have been delivered of your life-

---

15. Martin, *The Corinthian Body*, 232–33.

long sense of inferiority and shame.[16] You do not care if your veil slips and your hair falls down while the Spirit takes over your body as you pray in a tongue or prophesy a word from God. Indeed, your freedom and joy are so infectious you also draw in Deborah from the Cephas faction and Dionysia from Apollos's, who struggle with their own limitations as women in this society. What do you think about Paul's concerns in this passage and about the gender hierarchy he seems both to endorse and to transcend?

Those of Apollos—As upwardly mobile, respectable Corinthians, are you embarrassed by "those of Christ" who behave in unconventional ways at your worship services? How important is it to you that they listen to Paul and look like "proper" women? What do you think Apollos would say?

Those of Cephas—Wouldn't Peter think men *also* should have their heads covered when they pray? Isn't this your Jewish tradition? Think also of the women prophets in your history—Miriam, Noadiah, and Huldah—and other strong women like Deborah or Judith. What would they do in this situation?

Those of Paul—Are you torn by the same tensions as Paul regarding women's behavior in worship? Chloe, do you feel betrayed by Paul, or do you pick and choose what you like from what he says? Can you help the group decide what to do about what women and men wear during worship?

For everyone—Is Paul representing the facts correctly? Which of Paul's comments do you think are most important? What do you think of Paul's ranking of men and

---

16. Wire argues that the tension between the Corinthian women prophets and Paul arises from the differing impact of the new faith upon their status in society. For Paul, to be in Christ means to *relinquish status* as privileged, educated, and professionally recognized. For the women, to be in Christ means to shed a life of shame and to *claim a dignity and sense of authority* they had never known. "Reclaiming a Theology of Glory from the Corinthian Women Prophets," 40. For a fuller treatment of the subject, see Wire's *The Corinthian Women Prophets*.

women? Does Paul's argument change your mind in any
way? Why or why not?

Reader performs 1 Corinthians 11:2-16:

> *I commend you for remembering my instructions and
> keeping the traditions I passed on to you. However, I
> want you to know this, that the head of every man is
> Christ, and the head of woman is man, and the head
> of Christ is God. (11:1-3)*

> *A man who prays or prophesies with his head covered
> brings shame on his head, and every woman who prays
> or prophesies with her head uncovered brings shame
> upon her head. It is the same as if she had her hair
> shaved off. For if a woman doesn't cover her head, she
> ought to have her hair cut off. But if it's a disgrace for
> a woman to have her hair cut off or her head shaved,
> then she should keep her head covered. (4-6)*

> *A man should not cover his head since he is the image
> and glory of God, but woman is the glory of man.
> (For man was not made from woman, but woman
> from man. And man was not created for the sake of
> woman, but woman for the sake of man.) That's why
> a woman must have authority over her head, because
> of the angels. (7-11)*

> *However, in the Lord woman cannot do without man,
> nor can man do without woman, for as woman came
> from man, now man comes through woman—and all
> things come from God. (12)*

> *Think for yourselves: is it really proper for a woman
> to pray to God bare-headed? Doesn't nature itself
> teach you that for a man to wear long hair is shameful
> to him, but if a woman has long hair, it is her glory?
> For her hair is given to her as a covering. (13-15)*

> *If anyone wants to dispute this, they should know
> that we don't do it any other way, nor do any of the
> churches of God. (16)*

RESPONDING TO PAUL'S LETTER AS A HOUSE CHURCH

1. Let each faction share its reactions to Paul's perspective on how women wear their hair in worship. Who might object to men not covering their heads in prayer?

2. Which of Paul's comments about the relation between men and women do you think are most important? Is Paul representing the facts correctly? Should any changes be made in your house church in response to this text?

3. What do you propose your house church should do now about women letting down their hair as they pray and prophesy?

4. Paul stresses how he has "become all things to all people"—Jew, Gentile, slave, the weak (9:9-22). What evidence would you point to as to whether he is able to "become" a woman and see the subordination and head covering issues from a woman's perspective as well?[17]

DEBRIEFING AND APPLYING

1. Did this discussion arouse intense feelings—of freedom, timidity, anger, or joy?

2. How do you react to the view that in this passage Paul appears confused, and maybe even self-contradictory?

3. Are the views of the Corinthian women worth listening to today, or should we only pay attention to Paul's? Who better reflects the way of Christ?

4. One commentator notes that what prevailed in the church from this letter's discussion of male-female relations was not the message that both women and men had equal rights within marriage (7:2-5) or took leadership in worship (implied in 12:4-11; 14:3-5, 24-25, 29-33), but that women's role was secondary and subordinate to men's (11:3).[18] How does this echo through the church today? Who are today's women prophets?

---

17. This perspective is suggested by Lull, *1 Corinthians*, 100.
18. Bassler, "First Corinthians and Community Disagreements," 32.

15

HOW *NOT* TO EAT A "SUPPER OF THE LORD"

1 CORINTHIANS 11:17-34

When I (Reta) was teaching at Messiah College, I would eat meals with as many of my willing students as possible to get to know them better. One evening Lacey invited Jenna, Keith, and me to dinner in her apartment. During our conversation, Keith shared his fear of taking communion "unworthily" (1 Corinthians 11:27-29). So strong was his dread of God's judgment on him that he rarely participated in the Lord's Supper throughout middle and high school.

"Oh, Keith, do I have good news for you!" was my response—even as I lamented a theology that uses these verses as a club on tender consciences.

Perhaps this is why the Revised Common Lectionary used in most mainline churches only includes the story of Jesus' Last Supper (11:23-26) and omits the larger context (vv. 17-34) where Paul criticizes the Corinthians' meals. The Lectionary wants to be inclusive, not judgmental.

But when we omit the context, we misunderstand the reason *why* Paul recounted the story of Jesus' last meal with his disciples. He wants earnest believers like Keith to be included at the meal—but some Corinthians were excluding such people. Things were so bad, Paul says it would be better if they never met at all! (v. 17).

What is going on?

UNDERSTANDING THE BACKGROUND

We cannot answer this question without examining Greco-Roman meal practices. In Chapter 13, we took you to a meal of elite men at the local Asclepieion in Corinth. But there were many more private meals in homes to which friends, clients, and patrons were invited. Just as we today carefully set our table when guests are coming and pronounce a blessing over the meal, other such protocols were observed all over the Greek-speaking world.

Formal Greco-Roman meals. Jesus did not invent rituals of bread-breaking and sharing wine, even though he poured new meaning into them. A formal meal, usually held in the late afternoon or evening, would begin with the host breaking a loaf of bread to invoke the presence of the deity in whose honor they were meeting. Pagans might call upon lord Sarapis or the goddess Isis, and Jews would honor Yahweh. Christ-followers broke bread to remember Christ as their Lord.

Then they ate their meal. Not until "after supper," as Paul says in 11:25, did they mix the drinks. Water was always mixed with the wine;[1] then the first cup was poured out as an offering to the god or goddess. If the meal partakers were philosophers planning on a sober discussion afterward, they mixed more water with their wine. Those expecting lively entertainment and carousing used less water so they could get drunk.

Unless they were homeless, most people lived in small, upper-story rooms in tenement buildings. Some may have shared the rent with extended family or acquaintances in more spacious first-floor apartments, which often included shop space. Only the wealthiest owned freestanding villas.

The head of such a household would frequently invite male friends for dinner. It would be served in the dining room called a *triclinium*, which had couches lined up along the three walls opposite the door. Men would recline three to a couch, leaning on their left elbow and eating with their right hands from the meal served by slaves on low

---

1. With no refrigeration, fermented drinks like wine were their only option except when grapes were in season.

Upper Class Roman Villa

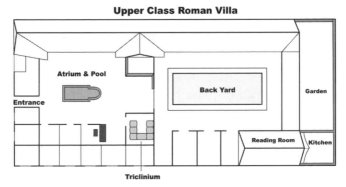

Even architecture in upper-class houses works against Paul's vision of eating together around the Lord's table. The dining room (*triclinium*) has three couches for nine diners. If the wealthier people eat before workers can arrive, the latter have to stand in the *atrium* and hope for leftovers.

tables. If a wife came along, she would sit on the couch beside her husband.

On one hand, eating together created a special tie among the diners and served to define boundaries between various groups. On the other hand, even for those within a particular group, one's age, gender, and status defined how one was treated at a meal. People sat or reclined according to their rank, and those of higher status even received food of higher quality. In the Roman mind, this made perfect sense. It contributed to the stability of the empire by reminding all persons that they should know their place and be content with it. Otherwise, confusion would result.[2]

As stated earlier, the highest value in Greco-Roman society was honor. Men continually tried to one-up each other in the public sphere. Though it was an honor to be invited to such a meal, the guests were now obligated to return the invitation at a later time. Their meals had to be at least as elegant as the one they had just enjoyed. Otherwise they would lose honor and status.

Jesus and table fellowship. All the Gospels, but especially Luke's Gospel, portray Jesus as a person who ate meals

---

2. Finger, *Of Widows and Meals*, 175–76; D'Arms, "The Roman Convivium and the Idea of Equality," 308–20.

with all kinds of people, whether or not they were ritually clean. In fact, Jesus' behavior at meals seems to have been the Pharisees' major criticism of him. They believed the kingdom of God would only come when God's people kept the law as perfectly as possible. As Jesus himself observed, they considered him a "glutton and a drunkard, a friend of tax collectors and sinners" (Matthew 11:19; Luke 7:34). Jesus' table fellowship with all the people of Israel, clean or unclean, poor or not-so-poor, was probably a major reason he got into trouble with the religious authorities. Not only did he break God's law, according to their perspective, but he also created social chaos. When people did not know their place and stay in it, the authorities feared it would cause social instability.

Paul and table fellowship. This message of social equality around the table was one Paul had brought to Corinth several years earlier. We do not know how he introduced it. He likely identified first with working-class Jews (see Acts 18:1-2) and then perhaps drew in other lower-class free and freed people and slaves. Perhaps wealthier people only joined the Jesus Movement later—maybe as a result of the preaching of Apollos.

But by now there are divisions in the Corinthian house assemblies, and they seem to be along class lines. As you listen to the reading of this text, there are many things to keep in mind:

- The better-off people are the ones who are able to provide space for the believers to meet regularly, since they have villas or apartments large enough to entertain groups.

- People of lower status are at a great disadvantage in participating in the common meals. Those of higher status draw their wealth from real estate and have slaves to do their work. They disdain manual labor. They often come together for a meal in the late afternoon so they have more time for discussion or entertainment. But all artisans, laborers, and slaves must work until the sun sets; they come to the evening meal and worship after work. By that time, the food may be gone. In 11:21, Paul says that "one goes hungry and another becomes drunk."

- The inequality is even more glaring since only the higher status people eat together in the *triclinium*. When the rest of the believers come, they must stand out in the *atrium* (entrance hall)—and only hope for leftovers from their patrons.

- This is likely a time of famine,[3] and, as always, high prices for food have the heaviest impact on the poor. Perhaps that is why they have no food to bring to the (supposedly) communal meals and are dependent upon wealthier patrons even for bread. This may explain verse 30: "this is why some of you are weak and ill, and some have died."

- Paul's main concern is that the believers are not eating *together* so that all have enough and are equal in status. He uses the Greek word for "come together" five times throughout this text.

- This is the only place in the New Testament where we find the term "the supper of the Lord." By this, Paul emphasizes the kind of communal meals Jesus used to have with all kinds of people (i.e., Luke 5:27-23; 7:36-50; 9:10-17; 14:7-24; 19:1–10; 22:19; 24:30). The wealthier Corinthian believers are *not* eating a Jesus-style supper; they are just eating their *own* suppers! (vv. 20-21).

- Paul quotes Jesus at his final meal before he dies—as does Luke in 22:19— saying, "This is my body that is for you. Do this in remembrance of me." Notice that neither text says, "Eat this."

---

3. See chapter 14 on 1 Corinthians 7:26. Winter, *After Paul Left Corinth*, 215.

Rather, it says, *"Do* this." *Share* this bread
with each other, just as I did with all people in
Israel. The same thing happens ("after supper")
with the cup. "This cup is the new covenant in
my blood. *Do* this, as often as you drink it, in
remembrance of me" (v. 25). *Share* this cup with
each other, as you saw me do so many times
before.

- Paul's harsh invective is surely directed at the
  patrons who have been behaving selfishly. His
  reference to the Lord's death and the bread and
  cup is to remind them that the Lord himself laid
  aside his status and privileges in order to share
  his life with those of no status—even if it meant
  his own death. Surely they can "proclaim the
  Lord's death" (v. 26) by dying to their privileges
  of when and how to eat.

- The poverty of many households is underscored
  by Paul's phrase, "as often as you drink [the
  cup]," indicating that many often cannot afford
  a cup of wine to drink (v. 25).

- Much of Paul's argument here hangs on the
  word into which he pours a double meaning:
  body. It means *both* Jesus' physical body *and*
  the body of believers. To share bread is to share
  bread with the body of Jesus now gathered
  in one place for a meal. For the higher-class
  believers to eat and drink without "discerning
  the body" (v. 29) is to eat and drink judgment
  against themselves. They are not only eating
  "their *own* suppers"; they are actively destroying
  the body. (In the following chapter, we will find
  more body language to drive this point home.)

- Two references to "eat at home" or "eat in the
  house" instead of with the body seem to detract
  from Paul's single-minded thrust (vv. 22, 34).
  Does this mean the higher-status believers should
  eat their richer food in private homes and then

serve bread to everyone at the communal meal? Paul cannot be speaking to slaves and working-class people because they do not own a house. Tenements do not have kitchens and certainly not refrigerators full of food. Slaves, of course, had no home to call their own.

When Paul uses the Greek word for "house" (*oikia*), he is referring to the *house church*, not to single-family homes like those we are familiar with.[4] The place to eat a full meal is with the entire house church. Paul's concern for the poor and hungry members of his Corinthian churches implies that these meals were expected to be regular, probably daily. Unless everyone eats *together*, and each *body* has enough calories, you are not meeting in honor of the Lord Jesus. Even Paul's constant use of terms like *brothers* and *sisters* should remind us of the nature of the new community as family.

Paul says to elite members, "when you come together to eat, *wait* for one another" (v. 33). But the Greek word translated "wait" (*ekdechomai*) is more forceful and means to "receive" or "welcome."[5] Not only wait for your supper, but also warmly welcome and honor every person who comes.

PREPARING FOR THE SIMULATION

Assume the meal is over in the *triclinium*, and a couple loaves of leftover bread have been circulated to the latecomers. Now everyone is gathered in the *atrium* to hear Paul's letter. Chloe can tell the house church that the next section is about their communal meals, and then give the factions a few minutes to discuss their current feelings about the meal with each other. Keep the background material in mind.

Those of Apollos—Even though there's been some grumbling and malicious rumors, you are quite comfortable with the way things are. One of you owns this house,

---

4. Henderson, "'If Anyone Hungers. . .': An Integrated Reading of 1 Cor. 11:17-34," 195–208.
5. Winter, *After Paul Left Corinth*, 151–52.

How Not to Eat a "Supper of the Lord"   169

so why shouldn't you and the other patrons eat as the Romans do? If your clients want more food, they can get here earlier or bring their own. You're already helping them with jobs and handouts. Besides, you think the most important thing about the meal is the spiritual part.

Those of Paul—You know something is not right: people aren't eating together since the group grew larger and moved the assembly to Erastus's house. You remember Paul's stories of Jesus' meals with many different kinds of people. If Jesus or Paul were here now, what would they think? Those Apollos people are just mimicking "the rulers of this age" (2:6). Several of your faction are absent because of illness.

Those of Cephas—You've had a bread-breaking ritual in your law-observant homes from little on up, where everybody was included. Peter taught us that at Jesus' meals even tax collectors and disreputable people were welcome. Whatever they do in that dining room, you're missing out on it. Besides, you're always hungry.

Those of Christ—You live on the edge of hunger, especially during this horrible famine. One of you actually died for lack of decent food, so you're really angry about getting only scraps at the Lord's table. Because you are caring for the sick or for children, or delivering babies, you often can't get to the meals until late. While you're not used to speaking up to people "better" than you, Paul has urged you to speak with the power of God, and you're desperate! You, house slaves, are expected to find enough food throughout the day as you work. But it's never enough. And you want to feel included with everyone else, like the Jesus-meals you've heard about.

Reader performs 1 Corinthians 11:17-34:

PAUL'S BIG DISAPPOINTMENT

*Now in what I say next, I do not commend you.
That's because when you meet together, it actually
does more harm than good! To begin with, when
you assemble together, I hear that there are divisions
among you; and I am convinced of this report. For
when you get together in one place, it is not really to
eat a Supper of the Lord. For when it comes to the
meal, some eat their own suppers first. The result is
that some go hungry and others are already drunk.*

*Really? Don't you have house churches in which to
eat and drink? Or do you show contempt for the
gathered church of God and humiliate those who
have nothing? What can I say to you? In this matter I
do not commend you!* (11:17-22)

EAT MEALS LIKE JESUS DID

*For I received a tradition from the Lord which I also
handed on to you: on the night the Lord Jesus was
betrayed, he took some bread. When he had given
thanks for it, he broke it and said, "This is my body
that is for you. Do this to remember me." In the same
way, after supper, he picked up the cup. He said,
"This cup is the new covenant in my blood. Every
time you drink it, do this to remember me." Every
time you share this bread and drink from a common
cup, you announce the Lord's death until he comes
back.* (23-29)

*This is why those who eat the bread and drink from
the cup inappropriately will be guilty of the body
and blood of the Lord. Reflect on your behavior, and
only then eat of the bread and drink of the cup. All
those who eat and drink* without understanding the
meaning of the body *are eating and drinking their
own judgment. This is why some of you are weak and
sickly. Some even have died!* (27-32)

So then, my friends, when you get together to eat, welcome each other. Let all the hungry people eat in the house church. Then when you gather together, it will not be for your condemnation. I'll give further instructions later when I come. (33-34)

RESPONDING TO PAUL'S LETTER AS A HOUSE CHURCH

1. Is there truth in Paul's accusations? If so, is he being unrealistic in this Roman Corinthian culture?
2. What is the central meaning of the Lord's Supper? Is it eating together as equals? Is it the act of sharing? Is it a personal experience of Jesus' continuing presence?
3. Are the poor and hungry justified in feeling angry?
4. How is the way of Caesar's empire different from the kingdom (kin-dom) of the Lord Jesus?
5. How does this conflict about the meal relate to Paul's distinction between the world's wisdom and the wisdom of God? (1:22-25).

DEBRIEFING AND APPLYING

1. What emotions arose for each of you in this reenactment?
2. If this interpretation of the Lord's Supper is accurate, how does it relate to the service of communion/Eucharist in your church or congregation?
3. What have contemporary churches lost by ignoring the social context in Corinth? How much additional teaching should we have regarding the ritual of bread and cup?
4. When was the last time you ate with someone from a different social class? Are our churches and private lives already so segregated that we never are challenged to eat across class lines?
5. For those of us who are middle-class, how do we "proclaim the Lord's death" by laying aside privileges of class and wealth?

16

SPIRITUAL GIFTS FOR THE SAKE OF THE BODY

░░░░░░░░░░░░░

1 Corinthians 12–14

Whether we act on it or not, most people would agree that regular physical exercise contributes to living a long and healthy life. Several years ago, I (Reta) started to notice the expression, "What's good for the heart is also good for the brain." I've been swimming three miles a week for over thirty years, so maybe something that I knew was good for my heart can also keep my brain healthy.

The apostle Paul knows nothing of modern medicine, but he understands the need for all parts of one's body to work together. And as we saw in the preceding simulation, he insists that the corporate body of Christ will be destroyed unless every single body eats together with all other bodies in that body, so that all have enough.

Although we are dividing 1 Corinthians 11–14 into three simulations, they are all part of Paul's theology of community worship. As long as the early believers meet in private homes, their practice is to gather for a common meal, followed by a time of worship and teaching.

We do not know whether the practice of prophecy and speaking in tongues was widespread in the early Jesus Movement. Paul says nothing about tongues in other letters, possibly because their use was not a problem. But it

172

troubled some in Corinth enough to ask Paul for advice in the letter they sent him. Thus Paul begins chapter 12 with the same phrase, "now concerning . . ." (12:1) that he used three times before to discuss a topic the Corinthians themselves raised (7:1; 7:25; 8:1).

UNDERSTANDING THE BACKGROUND

Who would curse Jesus? Declaring that "Jesus is cursed" (*anathema*) may seem odd to us, but ordinary Corinthians would naturally assume that about a man crucified by the Romans as a common criminal. Only those believers baptized into God's Spirit can proclaim the ironic, countercultural reality that "Jesus is Lord" (12:3).

Does the body illustrate hierarchy or equality? Greco-Roman society believes that the physical body is a hierarchy of honor, with the head having the most honor and the feet the least. Using the body as a metaphor to promote social stability is quite common in this culture. When lower classes would protest and demand more rights from the aristocracy, leaders would use the body metaphor to stress that all parts of the civic body must perform their proper roles—and stay in their place.[1] This of course perpetuates hierarchy. Paul, however, makes the *opposite* point in 12:12-26—that the hidden body parts are, if anything, more important than the ones we display.

Is "apostle" a high-status role? In 12:27-30, Paul seems to revert to hierarchy when he lists roles in the body of Christ. This may be merely a chronological description, where apostles precede other workers in order to plant a church.[2] Or perhaps it is a status reversal, since by the standards of normal society, apostles were low status. They are only servants and farm laborers (3:6-8) and the scum of the earth (4:9-12).[3]

---

1. For a fuller discussion of the use of body imagery, see Mitchell, *Paul and the Rhetoric of Reconciliation*, 157–64, and Martin, *The Corinthian Body*, 92–96.

2. Hays, *1 Corinthians*, 217.

3. Martin, *The Corinthian Body*, 102–3.

Bodies in love—Paul's "wedding sermon." Most of us have heard wedding meditations centered on the "love chapter" of 1 Corinthians 13. This is appropriate, of course. Unselfish *agape* love will be the main cement holding a marriage together when feelings of romance and *eros* get buried under the stresses of everyday life. But in Paul's letter this *encomium*[4] to love is about abuses that Paul sees in the strife-torn house churches in Corinth.[5] True love for the whole body means sacrificing personal privileges, laying aside irritations, and having one's own way. By providing an overall rationale in chapters 12 and 13 before getting into details, Paul tries to come across as tactful and nuanced.

Lost in translation—and other literary puzzles. In 13:1, the "noisy gong" should be translated "an echoing bronze (*chalkos*)." Corinth was noted for its bronze vessels and statues. Recall how in our chapter 2 Babbius Italicus boasts about his bronze products. This may refer to the bronze acoustic vases used in the theater to amplify the voices of the actors.[6] The "clanging cymbal" was associated with the cult of Cybele, a mystery religion known for its wild ecstatic worship practices.

"If I hand over my body so that I may . . . boast"? A Greek word in 13:3 is unclear and may mean either "burn" or "boast," since these words are identical except for one letter. "Boast" is the more difficult translation, so it is more likely that a copyist changed it to "burn" later, rather than the reverse.

What are tongues-speaking and prophecy? Speaking in tongues (*glossolalia*) is speaking or praying in an unknown language in worship, which presumably comes directly from the Holy Spirit and not through the mind of the person speaking. Prophecy in this context is an insight or exhortation from a Scripture passage that comes to

---

4. A formal text that expresses high praise.
5. It functions like 1 Corinthians 9 does in the middle of the discussion of idol-meat and demonic banquets (chaps. 8 and 10).
6. Murphy-O'Connor, *St. Paul's Corinth*, 75–77.

a person which she may not have thought about on her own. It is an intelligible message applicable to a particular situation being discussed or prayed about.

A word of prophecy seems to have been quite common in the earliest Christian communities. Peter quotes the prophet Joel (Acts 2:17-18) at Pentecost to announce that God would no longer speak selectively to certain prophets (like Isaiah or Jeremiah in the Hebrew Bible). Now God's Spirit would enable even the most humble believer to speak words directly from God.

Silent women or prophesying women? The command to silence women in 14:34-36 is puzzling, since it directly contradicts women's praying and prophesying in 11:2-16. Scholars suggest various reasons why Paul may have included this statement. We agree with those who consider it a note (also known as a gloss) that a later copyist wrote in the margin, which subsequent copyists then inserted into Paul's text. But it must have been an early addition, since all known manuscripts include it, either after 14:33 or after verse 40. Such an insertion into an original text is called an interpolation. Note that if verses 34-36 were removed, the paragraph from 14:26-40 reads more smoothly and coherently.[7] The content of this particular gloss reflects a conservative trend restricting women's leadership that is also evident in 1 Timothy and Titus.

Preparing for the Simulation

Before hearing the text, participants should review their character descriptions to identify who performs which gifts, services, and activities listed in 12:4-11. Which ones are rated more or less honorable than others? All should consider how *agape* love is or is not manifested in the house church. Who receives or gives the most love?

---

7. Many scholars have weighed in on this problem. For example, Hays supports the interpolation thesis, *1 Corinthians*, 245–49. Horsley agrees, unless Paul is referring to married women (*1 Corinthians*, 188–89). Examples of those who reject interpolation and suggest a range of alternatives are Keener, *Paul, Women, and Wives*, 81ff., and Witherington, *Conflict and Community in Corinth*, 287–88.

The Corinthian Letters class at Eastern Mennonite Seminary introduce themselves as Chloe's house church in chapel (April 2011). This is the "Christ" faction composed of charismatic women slaves.

Those of Apollos— Literate people (like you) wrote to Paul about spiritual manifestations. Why? Do you see prophesying and speaking in tongues as evidence of your ability to access divine wisdom? Do those low-class prophesying women imitate you and take over the service until it gets out of hand? Would you challenge Paul on the way he reversed the traditional understanding of body imagery? How does your faction rank the offices and services in the church?

Those of Paul—You've been distressed at the worship services that seem to get out of control when people talk at the same time and when prophecies do not agree with each other. Who uses the dramatic spiritual manifestations to lord it over the others? Argue Paul's position about the church as a body of equality, as well as his specific instructions for orderly worship.

Those of Cephas—You've heard about Peter's Pentecost sermon and his quotation from your Hebrew prophet Joel (Acts 2). You know tongues and prophecy are gifts God gave to your own prophets. You are irritated that Apollonians think they derive from the wisdom tradition, or that some women prophets seem to merge them with their previous ecstatic worship in mystery religions. You want to show the others the proper use of tongues and prophecies; in this sense you agree with Paul on the need for order in worship.

Those of Christ—You love Paul's theology of the body! For all your low social status in this culture, use of tongues and prophecies are one way to help you show the others, especially the Apollos faction, that you have high status in

Christ. Those of you previously involved in a mystery religion find it easier than others to access the supernatural realm. Besides, such ecstasy helps you momentarily forget about your ordinary life of daily drudgery and abuse.

Reader performs 1 Corinthians 12-14:

MANY KINDS OF SPIRITUAL GIFTS

I know you have been concerned, brothers and sisters, about spiritual things. When you were polytheists, you worshiped idols. Since they couldn't speak, you spoke what you thought they were saying. But now, one way to tell if you are truly speaking through God's Spirit is that you will confess, "Jesus is Lord." You will never say, "Let Jesus be cursed"! (12:1-3)

In our house churches there are varieties of gifts expressed—but there is only one Spirit. There are varieties of services, but the same Lord Jesus. There are varieties of activities, but it is the same God who activates all of them—in everyone. The Spirit manifests itself in various ways through each of you for the common good. As a result, some speak wisdom; some speak knowledge; some express a deep faithfulness; some have the gift of healing or of working other miracles; some prophesy; some can discern spirits; some speak in tongues; and some interpret these tongues. (4-10)

EVERY PART OF THE BODY IS IMPORTANT

Just as each human body is a unit but has many different parts, in the same way we are members of the one body of Christ. We have all been baptized into this body—Jews or Greeks, slaves or free. We all drink of the same Spirit.

The human body has diverse parts for a purpose. Each part needs the other—to see, hear, smell, and so on. In fact, the members of the body that seem to be weaker or are hidden or are less respectable are

*absolutely indispensable. In fact, God has arranged
the body so that we give greater respect to what seem
like the inferior parts. This is so that our bodies work
together in harmony. You know that if you have a
toothache or stub your toe, your whole body hurts. If
you cannot see or hear clearly, it will affect everything
you do. On the other hand, if each part is working
well, you are able to appreciate and honor each
member. (12-26)*

*In the same way, each of you is a part of the body
of Christ. In the assembly, God has first appointed
apostles; second, prophets; third, teachers; then deeds
of power; gifts of healing; various kinds of assistance
and leadership; and various kinds of tongues. We
don't all do the same thing—but we should all strive
for the greater gifts. (27-30a)*

THE BODY WORKING TOGETHER IN LOVE

*So I will show you an even better way to work this
out:*

*If I speak in all human languages and the language of
angels, but do not have* agape *love, I am like an echoing bronze or a clanging cymbal. If I can prophesy
and understand all mysteries and all knowledge and
have enough faith to remove mountains, but do not
have love, I am nothing. (12:30b–13:3)*

*Love is patient and kind. It is not envious or boastful
or puffed-up or rude. It does not insist on its own
way, and is not irritable or resentful. It does not
delight in doing wrong but rejoices in telling the truth.
It bears all things, believes and hopes in spite of anything, and endures throughout everything. (13:4-7)*

*Love never ends. Prophecies and tongues and all
knowledge will come to an end. What we know and
prophesy today is only partial; when the complete
comes, the partial comes to an end. When I was a*

*child, my thinking and behavior were childish, but
after I grew up, I laid aside childish things. Now we
see as if looking into in a mirror; then we will see face
to face. Now I know in part; then I will know fully,
even as I have been fully known. There now remain
faith, hope, and love—but the greatest of these is
agape love. (13:8-13)*

Applying spiritual gifts with love in worship

*Now I want to explain how this love may be applied
in your worship services. You should desire the
spiritual gifts—especially the gift of prophecy. When
you speak in a tongue, it may spiritually encourage
you, but it's a foreign language to other people. But
when you prophesy, it builds up the entire church.
I'm happy for all of you to speak in tongues—but I'd
much rather you all would prophesy. Tongues only
build up the church if someone interprets. (14:1-5)*

*Actually, speaking in an unintelligible tongue is little
more than a lifeless flute or harp that isn't played
properly—or a bugle unable to call soldiers for battle.
If you really want to use spiritual gifts, work at
strengthening them to build up the whole church. If
you do have the gift of speaking in a tongue, pray for
the ability to interpret. That way you will both pray
and sing praise with your mind as well as with your
spirit. This will also communicate to outsiders. I'm
glad I speak in tongues more than all of you—but
in the assembly I'd rather speak five words with my
mind than ten thousand words in a tongue. (6-19)*

*If your whole church comes together, and you all
speak in tongues at the same time, outsiders or unbelievers who visit or overhear will think you sound
like the frenzied worship of a mystery religion. But if
you prophesy in our common language, outsiders will
understand, the secrets of their hearts will be dis-
closed, and they will worship God and declare, "God
is really among you!" (23-25)*

THE DETAILS OF WORSHIP

*My brothers and sisters, here's what you should do.
When you come together, each one shares a hymn, a
revelation, a tongue, or an interpretation. Whatever
you do, do it to build up the whole church. No more
than two or three people should use a tongue—each
in turn—and then let someone interpret. If no one
is there with the gift of interpretation, no one uses a
tongue. Let only two or three prophets speak, and let
others consider what is said. If a revelation comes to
someone else sitting nearby, the first speaker should
stop talking. If you go one by one, everyone has a
chance to learn and be encouraged.*

*Those who prophesy in the Spirit are in control of
what and when they speak. God is not a God of
disorder, but of peace—as in all the churches of the
saints. Anyone who claims to be such a prophet, or
to have any such spiritual powers, must acknowledge
that what I am writing to you is a command of the
Lord. Anyone who doesn't should not be recognized
as a prophet.*

*And so, be eager to prophesy and do not forbid
speaking in tongues. But let it all be done decently
and in order. (26-33, 37-40)*

RESPONDING TO PAUL'S LETTER AS A HOUSE CHURCH

1. For those of you who do practice a spiritual gift
   of prophecy or speaking in tongues, what do you
   think of Paul's advice? Did you feel like he was
   speaking to you—or only to others who have
   been interrupting you during worship?
2. How would you prioritize the list of gifts,
   services, and activities in the church in 12:27-30?
3. In 13:4-7 Paul names eight behaviors that he
   says *agape* love is not: jealous, boastful, arrogant
   (puffed-up), rude, insisting on its own way, irritable, resentful, rejoicing in doing wrong. Where

and in whom have you seen these qualities in your house church?

4. In the same paragraph there are seven things that Paul says *agape* love is: patient, kind, rejoicing in the truth, bearing, believing, hoping, and enduring all things. Where and in whom have you seen this love expressed?

5. Do Paul's admonitions only refer to your communal worship, or also to the broader life of your house church? For instance, does he intend for higher-status persons to treat their slaves the same way they treat freed persons of equal or higher status? In chapters 12–14, Paul never mentions or names church leaders. Who is offended by that?

DEBRIEFING AND APPLYING

1. What was it like to play the role of either someone of low-status or of higher status? How emotionally involved were you? Were you defensive or repentant?

2. How might worship and congregational life be different if we took Paul's admonitions more seriously?

3. If we apply Paul's view of the body to our body politic, our life together as citizens, what would it mean? Who are the prophets of today calling us to bring selfless love, that is, social justice, into our civic and social structures?

4. How are tasks and responsibilities ranked in your church?

17

A FINAL CHALLENGE TO EARTHLY EMPIRES

∏∏∏∏∏∏∏∏∏∏∏

1 CORINTHIANS 15

"He's in a better place." "We'll miss her so much, but now she can be with her little sister and her father." "If you live right, you'll see him again." "Now she's with all her loved ones who have gone on before."

In a time of deep grief and loss, many Christians console themselves and each other with sentiments like these. Any of us over the age of eight knows we will never see the dead person alive on this earth again. But behind us lie centuries of human hopes that combine a confusing mixture of beliefs about the resurrection of the dead and the immortality of the soul.

In 1 Corinthians 15 we come to the climax of Paul's letter of ethical and theological advice to the house churches he planted several years earlier. Although Paul conveys certainty regarding his own eschatology (belief about death and the end times), the views of his converts are probably all over the map.

But first let us note how this long section functions in the letter as a whole. The text abruptly shifts from advice on ordered worship to "the good news that I proclaimed to you"(15:1). Except for closing remarks in chapter 16, this resurrection theology culminates Paul's argument about how Jesus' gospel should affect the lives and practices of the Corinthian believers.

All of Paul's practical advice in chapters 5–14 is framed by his theology of "Christ crucified" in chapter 1 and "Christ resurrected" in chapter 15. God's raising of Jesus' body vindicates the way Jesus lived his life and snatches victory from what would otherwise be a humiliating execution and political defeat. After burial, Jesus appeared to his disciples, who then had to rearrange their entire worldview to make room for this unexpected event (15:5-8). Did this mean that God's Messiah had come, and Rome was not all-powerful after all? That Jesus' nonviolent challenge to the domination system was more effective in the long run than attacking it violently? That they must continue living out Jesus' own patterns of friendship and self-emptying? Would the resurrected Jesus give them courage to face the powers of this world?

There is no doubt Paul believes this. Why else would he suffer so much to proclaim the gospel? (15:30-32). Why else would he repeatedly call for the elite members of his house churches to give up precious privileges of their status-rewarding society? Paul argues that, as God in Jesus had identified with humanity bodily, so humans who are "in Christ" are called to partake bodily of his crucifixion (through cruciform living—renunciation of social privilege or endurance of suffering) and his physical resurrection. In the near future, Paul contends, Jesus will return to vindicate these small bands of followers. The "kingdom of the Lord Jesus" will vanquish the domination system of all earthly lords and empires—until Yahweh becomes all in all (15:23-28).

Paul reminds the Corinthians that he has already preached this message while he was with them (15:1-11). But he needs to repeat it because the present empire has pervaded the church in the form of inequality through patronage, social climbing, pulling rank, exploitation, and social discrimination—resulting in factions and quarrels and unnecessary suffering. This is *not* cruciform living. Without putting into action the upside-down gospel of "Christ crucified," there is no resurrection.

UNDERSTANDING THE BACKGROUND

Ancient views of death and afterlife. We know from the Gospels that Palestinian Jews at this time do not hold a uniform belief about physical resurrection (i.e., Matthew 22:23-33). The same would be true of Jews in the Diaspora. But at least since the Maccabean Revolt in the second century BCE, some Jews hold to bodily resurrection as vindication of faithfulness to Yahweh's law (i.e., Daniel 12:2-3). As followers of Peter, who had seen the resurrected Jesus, the Jewish faction in Chloe's house church would surely embrace a view similar to Paul's.

Probably the majority of Greco-Romans believe in no afterlife at all. A common inscription on a tombstone is "I was not, I am not, I care not"—used so often the Latin is abbreviated to NFNSNC.[1]

However, this is not universal. Since the time of Socrates and Plato, the concept of body/soul dualism would have also circulated in some form. "The soul lives forever, it is what gives life, and it has come down from God," writes one father on his son's tombstone. "The body is the soul's tunic."[2] Even some philosophers may have held to such platonic views at this time.

Among the masses, popular myths since Homer's time held that the dead live a shadowy existence in Hades.[3] And when some Corinthians heard Paul speak of believers rising from the dead, they may have thought of the god Asclepius, son of Apollo, whose healing center was in their midst and who had a reputation of restoring the dead to life.[4] Others may have dabbled in magic; some of the magical papyri of that time do speak of conjuring up the dead.[5]

But the educated, elite classes scorn ideas about bodily afterlife as ignorant and disgusting, like "resuscitating a corpse." Plutarch, a second-century Roman writer,

---

1. Cosby, *Apostle on the Edge*, 147; Martin, *The Corinthian Body*, 109.
2. Martin, quoting from a second century inscription, *The Corinthian Body*, 109.
3. Ibid., 109.
4. Ibid., 111.
5. Ibid., 111–12.

discusses the range of beliefs about what happens after death. He rejects the popular notion that "the lower-status . . . [physical] body could possibly attain the high status reserved for the more subtle, purer substances of the self."[6]

Thus we can see that less-educated people who believe in such myths and magic would have found it easier to accept Paul's doctrine of bodily resurrection, even if Paul's Jewish eschatology implies something very different.

"Are we already resurrected?" Two references in other Pauline letters refer to an early theological misunderstanding. In one, Paul corrects those who think the "day of the Lord is already here" (2 Thessalonians 2:2), and in the other, the writer criticizes two men who "have swerved from the truth by claiming the resurrection has already taken place" (2 Timothy 2:18). Some scholars think this is also an issue in the house churches of Corinth. However, given Paul's stress on the physical body, it is more likely that what some Corinthians "found objectionable about some of Paul's teaching was not the *future* aspect of the resurrection but that it was to be a *bodily* resurrection."[7]

Body language in Paul's letter. As if to prepare for his rhetorical climax on bodily resurrection, Paul stresses the importance of the physical body throughout his letter. Men must not visit prostitutes because "the body is for the Lord and the Lord is for the body . . . Your body is a sanctuary of the Holy Spirit within you" (6:12-20). Paul gives great attention to marriage, sexual union, singleness, circumcision, and literal bodily slavery (7:1-40). Food is crucial for *all* the bodies in the house church (11:17-34), and what we eat and with whom has spiritual implications (chapters 8 and 10). Body language pervades chapter 12 as Paul describes the body of Christ in physical terms.

An early confession in 15:3b-5. Paul most likely received this confessional statement ("Christ died for our sins

---

6. Ibid., 114.
7. Ibid., 106.

This tomb with rolling stone just outside Jerusalem is similar to the type of tomb in which Jesus was buried.

according to the Scriptures . . .) from the original apostles, the ones he mentions in verses 5-7. This may date back to Paul's first meeting with the apostles after his conversion, perhaps within three years after Jesus' crucifixion.[8] This confession stresses that Jesus was really dead and was buried. Yet after the third day in the tomb, people begin to see him again. Against all expectations, it now dawns on them that Jesus' resurrected body proves he is the messiah Israel has longed for.

Only "some" Corinthian believers say there is no resurrection of the dead (15:12). Who are they? As stated above, these are probably the more educated, worldly-wise members—those who "belong to Apollos." But without physical resurrection, argues Paul, we have no gospel; it's the bedrock on which everything else is built. Without Jesus' resurrection, "your faith is futile, and you are still in your sins" (15:17). This last clause reminds us that Jesus' death alone cannot remove sin. God condemned Jesus' unjust execution by raising him to life. Otherwise he is just another failed messiah.

---

8. Hays, *1 Corinthians*, 255.

A new twist to the original confession. Paul is the earliest writer (see 1 Thessalonians 4:13-18) to connect Jesus' resurrection with God raising those who are "in Christ" at a later time. Jesus is the "first fruits" (15:20) of the new age. Many Jews believe in a general resurrection at the end of this age. To Paul, Jesus' resurrection means that this age is now coming to an end, and the new age is breaking into history with major political consequences. It means the end of the client-kings of the Herod dynasty in Palestine, the end of the corrupt temple system, the end of the Roman Empire itself, with its arrogance and class hierarchy and domination by a privileged elite! Paul must be aware that this conviction, if widely believed, will prove to be a direct threat to those presently holding power.

Paul also assumes his readers know Genesis 1–3. Jesus is the "new Adam" who goes back before Rome to the beginning of human history to reverse the sin and death the first Adam brought into the world.

Baptism for the dead. Other than Mormons,[9] few claim to know what baptism for the dead means. But at least some must have been performed within the Corinthian community. Paul uses the practice as another argument for resurrection: why do it if there isn't any?

What kind of body is the resurrection body? The paragraph that deals with this question (15:42-49) is often misunderstood. We "get" Paul's analogy of a plant not resembling the seed it grows from in the ground. What trips us up is where Paul says in verse 44, "It is sown a physical body, it is raised a spiritual body" (NRSV). Other English translations use the terms *natural* and *spiritual*. Either way, readers often assume that a "spiritual body" is an oxymoron, or that there will not be a bodily resurrection after all—that only our spirits will exist in the future.

What Paul actually says in Greek is "*psychikon* body" and "*pneumatikon* body." This confusion arises because

---

9. For example, they have a pool in their temple in New York City used specifically for baptism for the dead.

these terms are very hard to translate concisely. A *psychikon* body is a natural, mortal body like ours today.[10] This is the "natural" human being who will live and eventually die. What Paul means by a *pneumatikon* body is a resurrected body that will be just as substantial and physical as our present bodies. But these bodies will be so animated by God's Spirit that they will never die again.[11] The solid, material, resurrected bodies of those "in Christ" will be kept alive forever by the same Spirit that raised Jesus from the dead.

Ethical conclusions. On the basis of the resurrection, Paul urges ethical behavior in the present (15:33-34, 58). Our certain hope for the future should shape how believers live each day. In this Corinthian context, Paul says, it surely means to:

- renounce privileges or share them with the body of Christ;

- respect others' consciences;

- eat together so all have enough;

- submit your grievances to the judgment of each other;

- shun the "tables of demons"—idolatrous public banquets;

- let all speak in the common worship services;

- practice cruciform living.

PREPARING FOR THE SIMULATION

Those of Apollos—As the most educated members of the house church, you also see yourselves as the most spiritually mature. You may be among the "some" who say

---

10. Paul alludes here to Genesis 2:7 from the Greek Septuagint (LXX) where God breathes into Adam and he becomes a *psychē zōsan*—a living being, or a living soul.

11. Hays, *1 Corinthians*, 272.

there is no resurrection of the dead (15:12). You do not believe in the myths of Asclepius or of any other god raising corpses to live again; the idea sounds disgusting. Some of you may believe that when you die, your souls will go to heaven to be with Christ forever while your body will decay in the ground and disappear. You are skeptical of Paul's radical view of bodily resurrection because it implies that the social order will be turned upside down—to your detriment.

Apollos himself did not exactly support your present view, but the eloquent way in which he had preached while in Corinth made him sound to you like a real philosopher who was more interested in talking about the Spirit than about bodily matters.

Those of Paul—You usually go along with Paul's theology; he's your favorite preacher. And Fortunatus and Achaicus have spent enough time with Paul in Ephesus to be convinced, even if it goes against their former assumptions about body and spirit. Chloe (and Phoebe) generally agree, although they are older and more educated, so Paul's view is still somewhat of a struggle to accept.

Those of Cephas—For followers of Peter, Paul's argument makes sense, even though Peter has not yet come to such sweeping political conclusions. Your former belief in bodily resurrection now has more evidence and certainty.

Those of Christ—If Paul is right, the news is almost beyond belief. As lower-class women or slaves, you know what it is like to be simply "a body." You exist in this culture not to think and reason, but to do whatever you are told. Yet among this body of believers, you have been transformed into thinking persons who now exhibit many spiritual gifts. After you die, do you want this abused body of yours to be made alive and perfect? You welcome the day when the Caesars and all your exploiters will meet their match, and Christ will destroy all these "enemies of life—every other ruler, authority, or power" (15:24-27).

Reader performs 1 Corinthians 15:1-58:

EVIDENCE FOR JESUS' BODILY RESURRECTION

As a climax to this letter, brothers and sisters, I want to remind you of the core Good News. It's what I received, what I passed on to you, and it's the saving foundation upon which you stand. (15:1-2)

I handed on to you the most important news I had received: that the Messiah died for our sins according to the Scriptures, that he was buried, and that he was raised on the third day, according to the Scriptures. Then he appeared to Peter, then to the twelve original disciples, then to more than five hundred brothers and sisters at one time—most of whom are still alive. Then he appeared to James, then to all the apostles, and last of all to me. But no matter which of these witnesses came to you, this is how you came to believe. (3-11)

JESUS' RESURRECTION AS THE FIRST FRUIT OF THE DEAD BEING RAISED

Now if we all affirm the Messiah has been raised from the dead, how can some of you say there is no resurrection of the dead? The raising of Christ from death and the raising of those who have died in Christ are integrally connected. If the one did not happen, the other will not happen, and vice versa. If our hope relates to this life only, we are deluded and of all people the most to be pitied. (12-19)

But in fact Christ has been raised from the dead, the first fruit of those who had died. Death came into the world through human beings, Adam and Eve, and so the resurrection has also come through a human being, Messiah Jesus. (20-22)

But there will be a specific order of events. Christ was raised first, then when he returns, all those who have died in him will be raised. Then he will destroy all the enemies of life—every other ruler, authority, and power. The last of those enemies is Death itself. At last the Son will subject himself to the One who created all things, so that God may be all in all. (23-28)

Look at your own practices. If there is no resurrection of the dead, why do some of you receive baptism on behalf of the dead? And why do I and my companions go through danger every hour of the day? Why do I "fight with wild animals" in Ephesus if there is no hope of resurrection? Why not just "eat, drink, and be happy, for tomorrow we die"? Come to your right minds, brothers and sisters! You should be ashamed of yourselves. (29-34)

WHAT IS THE RESURRECTED BODY LIKE?

But some will ask: how does this work? Are corpses resuscitated? What kind of a body will resurrected persons have? Don't be foolish! New life cannot come without death. Think of the bare seed you sow in the ground. God gives a body to that seed, and each different kind of seed will produce a different kind of body. This is true for animals, birds, and fish, as well as stars and other celestial objects. (35-41)

It's the same for humans. The dead body that is sown in the ground will weaken and decay, but what is raised will be imperishable. It is sown a mortal body, but it will be raised an immortal body animated by God's eternal Spirit. It will have passed through death and come out on the other side. (42-44)

The physical and the limited came first, in Adam. He was made of dust. But now the Second Adam has a body of heavenly material that will not wear out. What I am saying is that our present composition of flesh and blood cannot ultimately inherit the kingdom of God. No, here's the mystery! In a moment, in the twinkling of an eye, the trumpet will sound, and the dead will be raised—and the living will be instantly changed. That which is mortal will put on immortality. (45-54a)

Then what is written will be fulfilled, "Death has been swallowed up in victory! / Where, O death, is your victory? / Where, O death, is your sting?"

The sting of death is sin, and the strength of sin is the law. But God gives us the victory through our Lord Jesus Christ. (54b-57)

Therefore, my beloved, be steadfast and always work for the Lord Jesus, for you know your labor is not in vain. (58)

RESPONDING TO PAUL'S LETTER AS A HOUSE CHURCH

1. What impact does this topic of resurrection have on you and your faction? Does it arouse hope, apprehension, or skepticism? What do you think it means for the future of the Roman Empire?
2. What was your pre-Christian view of what happens to the person after death? How was your perspective influenced by your social status? What, if anything, has changed since Paul, Apollos, or Peter introduced you to Jesus?
3. In what ways, if any, do you and your faction want to live differently from the secular Corinthian society because of the resurrection?
4. How do you understand Paul's statements about the body being mortal and then raised to immortality (15:44)? Would different factions interpret this differently?

DEBRIEFING AND APPLYING

1. How does Paul's view of bodily resurrection challenge common assumptions about the afterlife held among Christians today?
2. What does it mean for current power structures that Christ "will destroy all the enemies of life—

every other ruler, authority, and power"? What is the church's present role in this effort?

3. Paul wrote this letter before the concept of democracy replaced some totalitarian regimes in the world. How might Paul have stated things differently with democracy in mind?

4. Since resurrected bodies would live on a renewed earth (see Romans 8:18-25), what additional ethical concerns might Paul suggest today to prepare for the new age? Care for this planet? Adequate food and health care for all people? The distribution of the goods and wealth of the nation and the planet?

18

A CORINTHIAN
AGAPE MEAL

CAN'T WE DO BETTER?

■■■■■■■■■■■■■

Our walk through Paul's letter is now nearly complete.
What comes next? Let's imagine that the conversation in
Chloe's house church goes something like this:

> *"We've had quite a time together hearing Paul's
> letter read to us. We've heard Paul's words and
> we've had plenty to say ourselves. Our conversa-
> tions have revealed the tensions, the hard feelings,
> and the misunderstandings that have been plagu-
> ing us.*
>
> *"Shall we try to do better? Paul says we've been
> making a mockery of our common meal—treating
> the Supper of the Lord like an aristocratic impe-
> rial banquet. He wants to show the world what a
> community of love, faithfulness, and justice is like.
> Shall we start again—by waiting for each other
> and truly eating together?"*

UNDERSTANDING THE BACKGROUND

Nowhere in Corinth are questions of rank and status in
the domination system more evident than around food
and meals: where you sit, whether you recline or not, who
prepares the food, and even what you eat (see chapters
13, 15, and appendix 1). A few of you more privileged

urban plebes are accustomed to a diet of wheat bread, wine, some meat, and vegetables.

Many more of you rank among the poor, either as slaves, peasants, day laborers, or handworkers. Barley, rather than wheat, is the grain you mostly eat. Other staples include beans, peas, olives and olive oil, figs, goat's milk cheese, honey, and salted fish.[1] To supplement your meager diet, you are heavily dependent upon what is called "wild food," "famine food," or "barbarians' food." You forage for fruits, acorns, roots, and greens, or hunt small animals or fish in nearby streams.[2] Likely you have meat from domesticated animals only on feast days honoring the emperor and the gods, when meat offered to the gods is given out free.

What you bring to this meal should be appropriate to your economic status. For most of you, your rented room has no kitchen so you must find cooking facilities or an oven elsewhere if you need them. Buying from a food vendor is too costly. If you are better off, you can bring a dish with a small amount of meat. (See additional instructions in the Leader's Guide in appendix 2.) Besides the following list of ancient Mediterranean foods, you may choose from among the recipes at the end of this chapter.

What to eat and not to eat. If you are a Jew, or a Gentile who observes Jewish dietary laws, you will:

- Avoid pork, ham, bacon, rabbit, and camel (see Deuteronomy 14:3-8)

- Avoid reptiles and amphibians (see Leviticus 11:29-39)

- Avoid mixing meat with dairy products (see Exodus 23:19; 34:26; Deuteronomy 14:21)

- Drain all blood out of meat (see Leviticus 17:10-11; Acts 15:20)

- Avoid insects, except locusts (see Leviticus 11:20-23)

1. Day, *Your Travel Guide to Ancient Greece*, 69.
2. Kaufman, *Cooking in Ancient Civilizations*, 126.

- Avoid any meat that has been offered to idols.[3]

These are considered appropriate foods:

- *Grains*: (for the poor) flat breads, crackers and dishes using barley, lentils, and oats; (for the better off) wheat, pita, bulgur wheat

- *Vegetables*: beans, peas, chickpeas, onions, lettuce, squash, scallions, and most any other vegetable except tomatoes (not yet brought to the Eastern Hemisphere)

- *Fruits*: pomegranates, grapes, raisins, figs, lemons, oranges, dates, olives

- *Dairy*: eggs, cheese, yogurt, cottage cheese, ricotta cheese (preferably goat's milk but cow's milk acceptable)

- *Nuts and Seeds*: acorns (for the poor, chestnuts may be substituted), sesame seeds and most any nut

- *Beverages*: grape juice (diluted if you are poor), wine (usually diluted with two parts water; brought only by those who have no conscience against it)

- *Spices*: salt, pepper (only recently available), garlic, mint, coriander, thyme, and others

- *Oil*: olive

- *Sweetener*: honey, dates (not sugar, which is known only as a medicine)

- *Meat, Poultry, Fish*: (the poor will rarely have these unless they raised or caught them themselves) goat, lamb, mutton, chicken, fish, anchovies, beef

---

3. Adapted from Finger, *Roman House Churches*, 144.

A dramatic act: collecting funds for the Jerusalem church.
As we shall be hearing in 16:1-4, Paul strongly encourages
the Corinthian house churches to collect funds to send to
the believers in Jerusalem. A natural and ordinary gesture
today, this is highly unusual in Greco-Roman culture,
with its pyramid of hierarchical patron-client relationships in which wealth flows upward.

The collection Paul initiates, however, resists this pattern. It sends funds *horizontally* across provincial boundaries, from (primarily) Gentile believers in Corinth and
Galatia to Jewish believers in Jerusalem and Judea. Thus
the collection subverts the common customs of empire
and instead reflects the collegial and sacrificial values of
the coming reign of God.[4] Along with whatever other
motives he has, Paul is deliberately undermining hierarchical exploitation with a dramatic parable of "international" sharing. The future, Paul underscores, belongs
not to "the rulers of this age, who are doomed to perish"
(2:6), but to God's ways and wisdom.

PREPARING FOR THE SIMULATION

Phoebe, or the designated leader, may suggest in advance
that each faction think over what they can do to help the
house church reduce strife and better imitate the values of
Jesus. How might Paul's entreaty call them to repentance?

Those of Apollos—Much of Paul's verbal artillery has
been directed at you. You have been charged with elitism, sexual misconduct, bringing lawsuits against poorer
house church members, attending temple banquets, not
waiting to eat supper together, and getting tipsy at the
sacred meal. Can you relinquish your status privileges in
order to model Christ? Can you share with others in this
time of famine?

Those of Paul—Will you summon the courage to stand
up for what is right, even facing those of higher status?
Do you still have questions for Paul? Are those of you of
lower status ashamed to bring such meager food to the

---

4. Horsley, *1 Corinthians*, 220–24.

agape meal? Chloe, are there any privileges you feel called to renounce?

Those of Christ—How will you women prophets stand up in a loving way against Paul's rabbinic teaching about women's subordination? Is there any accommodation you want to make about wearing your hair down and being unveiled in worship? How about doing less speaking in tongues and paying more attention to orderliness in worship?

Those of Cephas—What changes of attitude regarding Torah teaching can you make for the sake of unity? Will you follow your conscience when eating kosher food without being intolerant of others? As circumcised children of God's original covenant, would you want to claim your special gift to teach the biblical accounts of God as liberator, to memorize psalms, and to warn against idolatry?

SHARING THE SUPPER OF THE LORD

Here is a suggested sequence for reenacting an *agape* meal (love feast)—a Supper of the Lord. It can be led by Phoebe, or any other designated person.

> **Setting out the food**
> **Prayer of thanksgiving**
> **Breaking the bread**
> **(quoting Jesus' words in 11:24)**
> **Sharing the food**
> **Sharing the cup (quoting Jesus' words in 11:25)**
> **Reciting a psalm**
> *How very good and pleasant it is when*
> *kindred live together in unity!*
> *It is like the precious oil on the head, run-*
> *ning down upon the beard, on the beard of*
> *Aaron,*
> *running down over the collar of his robes.*
> *(Psalm 133: 1-2)*
> *Give justice to the weak and the orphan;*
> *maintain the right of the lowly and the*
> *destitute.*
> *Rescue the week and the needy;*

A Roman *agape* meal followed the Corinthian chapel service at Eastern Mennonite Seminary. Enoch and Deborah (Irvin and Nancy Heishman) preside at the supper liturgy.

> *deliver them from the hand of the wicked.*
> *(Psalm 82:3-4)*

Prophecy: The four factions share how they can be more considerate for the sake of the unity of the body of Christ.

Prayers (under Chloe's and Phoebe's leadership)

Hymn (may be chanted or read together)

> *Though he was in the form of God,*
> *Christ Jesus did not regard equality with*
>   *God as something to be exploited,*
> *but emptied himself, taking the form of a*
>   *slave . . .*
> *He humbled himself and became obedient to*
>   *the point of death—even death on a cross.*
>   *Therefore God also highly exalted him*
>   *and gave him the name that is above every*
>   *name,*
> *so that at the name of Jesus every knee*
>   *should bend,*
> *in heaven and on earth and under the earth,*
> *And every tongue should confess that Jesus*
>   *Christ is Lord,*
> *to the glory of God the Father. (Philippians*
>   *2:6-11)*

Reader performs 1 Corinthians 16:

THE COLLECTION FOR JERUSALEM

Now I offer some directions about the collection for the Christians in Judea. (Actually, these are the same directions I gave to the house churches in Galatia.) Every Sunday I want each of you to set aside something, according to what you may have earned that week. Then there will be no need for collecting it all at once when I get there. When I arrive I will arrange to send your offerings to Jerusalem with those whom you choose, along with their letters of reference. If it seems worthwhile, I will go with them. (16:1-4)

TRAVEL PLANS AND FINAL INSTRUCTIONS

I will visit you after I travel through Macedonia, and I may stay for the winter, so you can speed me on my way to my next destination. I don't want to make a flying visit, but really want to spend some time with you, if the Lord allows me. For now I must remain in Ephesus until Pentecost, for even though there is much opposition, there is a great opportunity for me here. (5-9)

If Timothy comes, welcome him and make him feel at home and don't let anyone look down on him, for he is doing the Lord's work just as I am. Send him happily on his way back to us; I am looking forward to seeing him back along with the others. (10-11)

As for our brother Apollos, I strongly urged him to go to Corinth with the others, but he didn't feel he should go now. However, he will be seeing you when the right opportunity comes. (12)

Be on guard against spiritual dangers. Stand firm in your faith. Be brave and strong. Let everything you do be done in love! (13-14)

Now there is something else I ask of you, brothers and sisters. Remember how

Stephanas and his household were the first to become Christians in Achaia and generously put themselves at the service of God and the people of God. Follow their leadership and that of everyone who works so hard with them. I am so delighted that Stephanas, Fortunatus, and Achaicus have come here, for they have made up for my being away from you, and have encouraged me a great deal, as they do you. Be sure you show them your appreciation. (15-18)

GREETINGS AND A BLESSING

Greetings from the churches in Asia. Aquila and Prisca and the church that meets in their house greet you warmly in the Lord. All the brothers and sisters greet you. Greet each another with a holy kiss. I, Paul, am writing these greetings with my own hand. (19-20)

If any do not love the Lord, they bring a curse upon themselves; they are anathema. Maranatha, *our Lord is coming! The grace of our Lord Jesus be with you, as well as my love to all of you in Christ Jesus. (21-23)*

Invitation for comments on Paul's final chapter (optional)

Benediction

My beloved, be on guard against spiritual dangers. Keep alert, Stand firm in your faith. Be brave and strong. Let everything you do be done in love. Maranatha—*our Lord is coming!*

The grace of our Lord Jesus be with you. (1 Corinthians 16:13, 22-23)

DEBRIEFING AND APPLYING

1. How did this simulation feel in comparison to the others?
2. How successfully were the factions able to resist the elitist values of Corinthian society?
3. What parallel tensions are there in today's churches? Any examples?
4. Thinking about the simulation as a whole, what can you apply? How?

RECIPES FOR THE *AGAPE* MEAL[5]

Roman Lentil and Millet Salad
½ cup lentils
½ cup millet (or barley)
½ cup onion
¼ cup parsley
2 Tbsp. fresh mint
1 clove garlic
¼ cup lemon juice
1 Tbsp. red wine vinegar
1 tsp. salt

Simmer lentils in 1 cup of water for 20 minutes, or until soft. Simmer millet separately in 1 cup of water for 15 minutes. Put aside to cool. Mince onion, parsley, mint, and garlic. Add to grains. In a separate bowl, mix lemon juice, red wine vinegar, and salt. Pour over the salad and toss well. Top with freshly cracked pepper and drizzle with olive oil. (Millet is a sadly overlooked grain, mildly sweet and nutty. If hard to find, substitute barley.)

Lentils and Squash
1 butternut, acorn, or hubbard squash, diced
4 Tbsp. butter
1 cup brown lentils
salt and pepper to taste
1 large onion, sliced
1 Tbsp. lemon juice

---

5. Most of these recipes, based on ancient Roman foods, were adapted for our use by Carolyn Rothwell, caterer, Harrisonburg, Virginia.

¼ tsp. cinnamon
½ tsp. cumin

Halve squash, peel, remove seeds, and dice. Heat 2 Tbsp. butter in a skillet, sauté squash 3 minutes.

Add lentils, salt and pepper, and just enough water to cover. Simmer 20 minutes or until tender.

In another skillet melt remaining butter and fry the onion until tender and slightly browned. Stir onion, lemon juice, and cinnamon into the squash and lentils.

Eggs With Honey (*Ova Spongia*, in Latin)
4 eggs
3 Tbsp. honey
1 Tbsp. olive oil
1 cup milk
5 Tbsp. butter
sprinkling of black pepper

Beat together eggs, milk, and oil. Pour a little olive oil in a skillet and add the mixture. Cook like an omelet, then fold over and place on a platter. Warm the honey and pour over the omelet. Sprinkle with black pepper.

Greek Yogurt Salad
2 cups plain Greek-style yogurt
3 scallions, finely chopped
½ cup walnuts, chopped
¼ cup raisins
½ tsp. dried mint
3 radishes, grated
lettuce leaves

With melon-baller, shape yogurt into spheres. Arrange on bed of lettuce leaves. Mix all but radishes and sprinkle over yogurt. Top with grated radishes and serve.

Cold Yogurt Soup
2 cucumbers, peeled and seeded
3 cups plain yogurt
1 cup ice water
½ tsp. garlic powder

½ tsp. dried mint
salt to taste

Chop cucumbers very fine. Mix yogurt with ice water and pour over cucumbers. Add garlic powder, mint, and salt. Stir and serve.

Basic Bulgur
1 cup coarse bulgur wheat
2 Tbsp. olive oil
2 cups beef broth
salt and pepper to taste
1 tsp. parsley

Simmer bulgur wheat in beef broth; add salt and pepper. Cover and simmer 30 minutes or until bulgur wheat is tender. Add the parsley and olive oil. Stir and serve. You may add some chopped cooked beef.

Cabbage with Ginger
1 medium sweet onion, sliced
1 medium head of cabbage, shredded
3 Tbsp. butter
salt and pepper to taste
1 tsp. dry ginger or ½ tsp. fresh ginger (grated)
½ cup plain yogurt

Fry onion and cabbage in the butter with the salt and pepper and ginger for about 15 minutes or until tender. Dress with plain yogurt and serve.

Roman Libum (Cheesecake)
1 cup all purpose flour
8 ounces ricotta cheese
1 egg, beaten
4 bay leaves
½ cup honey

Sift flour into a bowl. Beat cheese until soft and stir it into the flour, along with the egg. Form a soft dough and divide into 4 buttered individual baking cups. Heat oven to 425°F. Place a bay leaf on top of each cake, cover cakes with foil and bake for 35–40 minutes until golden-brown.

Warm the honey and place the warm cakes in it so that they absorb it. Allow to stand 30 minutes before serving. Serves 4.

Roman Pear Patina
4 Bartlett pears, peeled and halved
2 Tbsp. honey
½ cup dessert wine
pinch of pepper and cumin
3 eggs
1⅓ cups milk (optional)
1 Tbsp. olive oil or butter

Poach pears in the sweet wine. Mash or blend pears and wine into a puree; add the eggs, milk, and spices with the olive oil. Pour into a buttered casserole and bake 20 minutes at 350°F. Serves 4.

Figs and Goat Cheese
1 package fresh figs
1 Tbsp. feta (goat) cheese for each fig
honey (optional)
pepper to taste

Wash and dry figs. Cut a cross slit in the top. Turn them upside down and mash them gently to "open." Stuff each with a Tbsp. feta cheese. Bake 10–12 minutes at 350°F. Sprinkle with pepper and pour honey over the top.

Chicken with Leeks (Only the wealthier could afford this dish.)
1 fresh chicken, cut up
1 stalk of leeks, washed and cleaned well
¼ cup olive oil
1 Tbsp. butter
salt and pepper
Fresh thyme

Season the chicken with salt and pepper; fry in olive oil and butter until tender. Sauté the leeks alone in a small pan until tender. Add fresh thyme and spoon over the chicken.

Poached Apricots
6–8 apricots
¾ cup white wine
¼ cup water
½ cup raisins
1 Tbsp. mint
2 Tbsp. honey
1 tsp. vinegar

Wash and pit apricots. Place in the wine and water. Add the honey, mint, raisins, and vinegar. Simmer 20 minutes. Remove apricots. Cook sauce until it thickens and serve over the apricots.

Roman Barley Cake
1½ cups barley flour
½ cup water
3 Tbsp. honey
2 Tbsp. olive oil
1 tsp. salt

Sift flour and add other ingredients. Form a ball. Cool in refrigerator 20 minutes. Roll as thin as possible. Cut in round shapes and bake on a greased cookie sheet 15 minutes at 400°F. While still warm, drizzle honey over the top or serve with goat (feta) cheese.

Hummus
2 cloves of garlic
30 oz. of canned chickpeas (drain well)
½ cup water
½ cup olive oil
2 Tbsp. lemon juice
¼ tsp. cumin
⅛ tsp. each of salt and pepper
¼ cup toasted pine nuts

Blend together until smooth. Drizzle a little olive oil over top and, if desired, put some chopped black olives on top. Put in a tight container. Keep cool. Spread on toasted pita bread.

Tabbouleh Salad
2 cups bulgur wheat
2 cups hot water
6 spring onions, finely chopped
1½ cups fresh parsley, chopped
2 Tbsp. fresh mint
½ cup olive oil
juice of 3 lemons

Add bulgur wheat to the hot water. Cover so steam cannot escape. Cool. Add all the ingredients to the cooled bulgur wheat. Stir well. Refrigerate.

Cold Vegetable Salad
1 small eggplant, peeled and cubed
2 large zucchini, cubed (do not peel)
1 bell pepper, cut into strips
1 stalk of celery, diced
1 clove garlic, finely diced
1 small hot pepper, finely diced and seeds removed (optional)
4 Tbsp. olive oil
1 Tbsp. butter
salt and pepper to taste
2 tsp. dried parsley
juice of ½ lemon

Sauté vegetables in olive oil and butter, adding garlic the last minute of cooking.

Add dried parsley and lemon juice. Cook another 5 minutes. Allow to cool. Chill and serve.

Baked Cheese Squares
1 cup sharp cheese, grated
1 cup flour (barley flour optional if you are poor)
1 cup milk
2 eggs
salt and pepper to taste
1 tsp. chives
2 Tbsp. butter

Mix all the ingredients and pour into a buttered 13x9 baking dish. Bake at 325°F for 30 minutes or until light brown on top. Serve as an appetizer.

Farina Diamonds
syrup: ¾ cup honey, ¾ cup water
3 eggs
1¼ cups farina (or Cream of Wheat)
½ cup chopped nuts
1 stick butter, melted

Simmer honey and water until warm and mixed together. Cool.

Beat eggs, add farina, nuts, and melted butter to the eggs, stirring well. Pour into a buttered 9x13-inch pan. Bake at 350°F for 30 minutes. Remove and after cooling cut into diamond shapes. Pour cooled syrup over the squares. (Pancake syrup can be substituted for the honey and water mixture.)

Green Peas and Basil
2 cups green peas (fresh or frozen)
2 Tbsp. chopped fresh basil or ¼ tsp. dried basil
salt and pepper to taste
¼ cup toasted pine nuts
1 Tbsp. olive oil
1 tsp. honey

Sauté peas in olive oil, making sure they are coated with the olive oil. Add just enough water to cover. Add the honey and salt, and bring to a boil. Reduce heat and simmer 5 to 8 minutes. Drain, sprinkle with basil and toasted pine nuts. Toss and serve.

Egg Salad
6 hard-boiled eggs
1 medium shallot or several green onions, sliced very thin
2 Tbsp. olive oil
juice of ½ lemon
1 Tbsp. honey
salt and pepper to taste
1 tsp. parsley or fresh basil chopped

Slice the eggs and lay on a platter. Place the shallot slices on top. Prepare the dressing of lemon juice, honey, salt and pepper, and parsley. Mix well, pour over the eggs, and serve.

Honey-Date Confection
1 cup shelled walnuts
black pepper to taste
20 dates, pitted
sea salt to taste
1½ cups honey

Chop the walnuts coarsely and sprinkle with pepper. Stuff each date with some of the peppered walnuts. Season with sea salt. Heat the honey in a saucepan. Simmer the stuffed dates gently in the honey for 10 minutes. Serve warm in the honey syrup. If desired, season with additional salt and pepper.

Sesame-Fig Treat
1 lb. dried figs
¼ cup sesame seeds, toasted in a 325°F oven for 5 minutes
2 Tbsp. fennel seed
2 tsp. cumin seed

If the dried figs are leathery, soften them a bit by poaching very briefly in boiling water. In a food processor combine all the ingredients to form a sticky, chunky puree. Roll into walnut-sized rounds.

Basic Beans
½ lb. dried fava (or lima) beans
3 Tbsp. olive oil
1 Tbsp. thyme leaves, minced
salt to taste

In a large pot, soak beans overnight, drain, then cook in fresh water about 20 minutes until tender. Or boil dry beans, then simmer and hour or so until tender. Drain, mix the beans with the olive oil, thyme, and salt and serve.

EPILOGUE

We have reenacted the reception of Paul's letter in a house church in Corinth. But what *really* happened? Did the letter settle the quarrels and divisions in the churches?

Fortunately, a trail of clues in both 1 and 2 Corinthians helps us reconstruct more of the tumultuous relationship between this apostle and his struggling congregations. However, the trail is not easy to follow because 2 Corinthians seems to be a collection of several letters—not necessarily in chronological order.

As we have gradually absorbed Paul's radical vision of what God was doing in the world through his Messiah Jesus, we realize what Paul was up against. His insistence on lifestyle changes must have been very difficult for those who were accustomed to the values and structures of the domination system of the Roman Empire. Indeed, in the months after Paul wrote 1 Corinthians, he experienced an enormous challenge to his leadership and authority. Soon after he sent the letter, he dispatched his companion Timothy, with some anxiety, to see how things were going (1 Corinthians 16:10-11). This was his second visit, since he had earlier been treated with contempt (1 Corinthians 4:17-18).

Timothy's second visit must not have been successful either, because Paul himself changes his plans in order to briefly visit Corinth again—but he is apparently insulted and humiliated by at least one person during that visit (2 Corinthians 1:23–2:11). Rather than returning and risking more personal confrontation, Paul writes a conciliatory "letter of tears" (2 Corinthians 2:4), which he sends with another coworker, Titus. (That letter appears to be lost.) When Titus returns with good news of the Corinthians' apology and repentance (2 Corinthians 7:5-17), Paul is overjoyed.

TROUBLE WITH "SUPER-APOSTLES"

Nevertheless, challenges to Paul's leadership continue because of other church leaders—Paul calls them "super-apostles" (2 Corinthians 11:5)—who are making inroads into the Corinthian assemblies. They belittle Paul, saying, "His letters are weighty and strong, but his bodily presence is weak, and his speech is contemptible" (2 Corinthians 10:10). Paul responds with what we call 2 Corinthians 10–13, in which he uses irony and sarcasm to defend his upside-down ministry of God's strength working through human weakness and suffering.[1]

The "patronage pyramid" described in Chapter 7 of this book and Paul's forceful argument in 1 Corinthians 9 against accepting financial support from patrons help us to better imagine the cause of such conflict. Paul is convinced that Jesus' gospel requires believers to share or lay aside whatever privileges they have which keep them from serving the common good in the body of Christ. Although he has a right to financial support in his apostolic work, he refuses it to become a lower-class manual laborer (Acts 18:1-2). He rejects patronage so he is not obligated to those with wealth at the expense of the working classes. Clearly, the "super-apostles" *do* accept patronage, so they are honored while Paul is put down.

CLUES OF RECONCILIATION

It appears, however, that Paul did make the longer visit that he had promised in 1 Corinthians 16:5-7. He appar-

---

1. Though we know Paul had an extended relationship with his Corinthian churches through letters and visits, an exact chronology is always hypothetical. Two chronologies with a few differing details can be found in Shillington, *2 Corinthians*, 17–19; and Barr, *New Testament Story*, 131. Barr suggests 2 Corinthians 10–13 may be the "letter of tears."

ently makes peace with his contentious house churches because he writes to the Roman Christians from Corinth within the next couple of years. He stays at the home of Gaius, a house church leader (1 Corinthians 1:14; Romans 16:23). The secretary Tertius transcribes the letter that he dictates. Both of them, along with Erastus, send greetings to believers in the capital city. In this letter there is no hint of the past history of struggle and tension.

ACKNOWLEDGMENTS

George McClain and I (Reta) both know that this book is better than it would have been if only one of us had created it. George has been an enthusiastic and gracious partner—as well as a relentless editor! I am very grateful for a friend and colleague who both challenges and cheers me on.

We were still writing chapters of this book in 2011 when I began teaching a course called "Corinthian Letters" at Eastern Mennonite Seminary, Harrisonburg, Virginia. The thirteen students of Chloe's house church were highly engaged and interactive in our simulation, making this one of the most fun and exciting courses I have ever taught! I gained as many new insights as did the class. I wish to thank these students in their respective factions, chosen by lot:

- Those of Paul—Philip Showers, Richard Barton, Jossimar Diaz-Castro

- Those of Apollos—Tammy James, Byron Pellecer, David Stenson, Jared Stoltzfus

- Those of Cephas—Irvin Heishman, Carl Van Stavern, Melissa Fletcher Zook

- Those of Christ—Nancy Heishman, Kara Yoder, Rebecca Van Stavern

I'm grateful for the Sunday school class at Community Mennonite Church, Harrisonburg, Virginia, who faithfully participated in this simulation during the Winter Quarter, 2011–12. We averaged eighteen to twenty participants each week, creating a successful simulation. I appreciate our pastors, Jennifer Davis Sensenig and Steve Schumm, who centered five worship services around 1 Corinthians so this study could become a learning experience for the whole congregation.

Lastly, I thank my graphic artist son Ted Finger, who took time to create the floor plan of a Roman house, which suggests how abuses at the Lord's Supper occurred. And a friend, Carolyn Rothwell, used her cooking expertise to adapt Roman recipes for potluck *agape* meals.

For my part, I, (George) am deeply indebted to Reta Finger for pioneering this genre of simulation of Paul's house churches in her earlier *Roman House Churches for Today* and for her partnership in this endeavor. I could not ask for a more dedicated, collegial, and inspiring writing partner.

I am grateful to students in a variety of academic settings whose willingness to test various models of Corinthian simulation (mostly in costume!) have taught me so much: successive cohorts of Doctor of Ministry students at New York Theological Seminary; semiannual courses in the Theology of Mission for United Methodist deaconess and home missioner candidates (through New York Theological Seminary); New Testament classes in the Rising Hope, Inc., Certificate Program in Ministry and Human Services at Arthur Kill Correctional Facility in Staten Island, New York; and gatherings of the Prayer House Community, Dingman's Ferry, Pennsylvania. In each setting participants have helped bring to life the characters in this reenactment and further instructed me in the remarkable relevance of Paul's letter for ministry today.

I also want to acknowledge the careful and caring support—editorial, technical, and spiritual—that I've received from my dear spouse, the Reverend Tilda Norberg, my wise children, Shana Norberg-McClain and Dr. Noah Norberg-McClain, and our most capable assistant, Jennifer McCue.

Finally, we express our deep appreciation for the assistance of editor Byron Rempel-Burkholder and his colleagues at Herald Press/MennoMedia.

APPENDIX 1

ARROGANT ARISTOCRATS IN ACTION

𐃘𐃘𐃘𐃘𐃘𐃘𐃘𐃘𐃘𐃘

CORINTH'S ELITE GATHER AS THE ISTHMIAN GAMES BEGIN—A REENACTMENT

At the close of chapter 2, our Corinthian tour guide, Babbius Italicus, invited us to an evening reception at the temple of Asclepius. Babbius introduced us to a colony of Rome planted on the site of a conquered Greek city. It has the basic features of Rome itself—a theater, magnificent public buildings, a main square, many elegant statues, gushing springs feeding the baths, numerous temples and shrines, as well as shops and eating places. Maybe you didn't see latrines, but they are there too. Corinth at mid-first century is an impressive outpost of Rome itself and a crossroads for commercial activity, as well as culture and language.

Just as important are the values and behaviors of elite Corinthians. This reception—which we shall act out—will dramatize attitudes and behaviors of those with power and authority. This drama is made up but is historically plausible, using actual events and characters as much as possible. Those who are not slaves are historical persons from that period, acting typically from what we know about them. The actual lives of slaves, of course, have left little trace.

A common behavior at this time is the practice of boasting, which historians tell us the Corinthians took to

215

extremes. Intensely competitive, elite Corinthians highly prized rhetoric, flaunted their wealth, and enthusiastically displayed their piety in public—whatever they may have thought privately.

THE SETTING

The Panhellenic Games sponsored by Corinth are a major focus of Corinthian life and a major attraction for all of Greece. There are four major games: at Olympus (ancestor of our Olympic Games), Nemea, Delphi, and the Isthmian Games sponsored by Corinth, which take place on the isthmus connecting mainland Greece with the Peloponnese. Their fame is second only to those at Olympus, held near the mountaintop home of the goddesses and gods. But the Isthmian events probably attract more attendees because they are much nearer to population centers and accessible by sea, the preferred means of long distance travel. Contestants come from all over Greece to participate. The Isthmian Games are at once athletic contest, cultural showcase, amusement park, and religious festival. (See chapter 7 on Greco-Roman religions.)

Our scene takes place on the evening before the games begin in the spring of the year 54 CE, the same year the Jesus followers in Corinth receive a letter from the apostle Paul.

In our scene, the president of the games, Julius Spartiaticus, who occupies the most prestigious post in the city, is holding a reception for the Corinthian power structure on the evening before the games begin. The grand marshals who have been in charge of organizing the games will introduce the guests to the feature events they have planned.

The reception is being held in the "medical center" of Corinth. This is a complex known as the Asclepieion, the sanctuary of the much-beloved god of healing, Asclepius, son of Apollo. His shrine was established long ago in Corinth and was one of the first buildings to be repaired when Julius Caesar established the Roman colony of Corinth one hundred years after Greek Corinth's earlier destruction. The sick come from many miles around to sleep overnight in a special area (the Abaton) and have their healing dreams interpreted by the priests and physicians of Asclepius. The temple complex also has a series of elegant banquet rooms opening out onto a colonnaded portico, and it is here that the Games President Julius Spartiaticus is, at his expense, holding a much-anticipated reception for local notables. In an unusual move, Spartiaticus has let it be known that the new Roman governor and the mayoral team will be delivering some special pronouncements.

THE CHARACTERS

1. Roman governor: **Atticus Antonius** just arrived a few months ago, newly appointed governor of Achaia (Greece). He is from an old Roman noble family. He previously served as governor of a less prestigious province and is a favorite of Emperor Claudius.

2. President of the Year 54 Isthmian Games: **Julius Spartiaticus**, whose distant ancestors were from Sparta, has been duovir *quinquennalis* (mayor plus administrator of the census held every five years) in years 47–48 and again in 52–53 CE.

3. Grand marshal for day 1: **Claudius Optatus**, leading manufacturer of Corinthian bronzes. He is quietly campaigning to be elected duovir for the next year. The mayor's position is held jointly by two people elected to serve together for a one-year term.

4. Grand marshal for day 2: **Ventidius Fronto**, young and ambitious, hopes to be elected duovir in a few years.

5. Grand marshal for day 3: **Babbius Italicus**, prominent among the local elite, known to us as our tour guide.

6. Grand marshal for day 4: **Julius Polyaenus**, the retiring *Pontifex Maximus*, the highest-ranking priest. He, too, is hoping to be elected duovir in the next year.

7. Games assistant: **Domitian Quadratus**, not a member of the elite, but highly trusted to administer events on their behalf. Actually born a slave, he purchased his freedom with income from his work as a scribe. He is a devotee of the god Mithras.

8. **Junia Theodora**, a quite remarkable woman from Lycia (across the Aegean Sea), who has been heaped with tributes for facilitating relations between Lycia and Corinth.

A class of aspiring United Methodist deaconesses role-play aristocrats at a banquet on the eve of the Isthmian Games.

9. **Claudius Dinippus** has served twice as *curia annonae*, a special emergency post created to address serious grain shortages in times of famine.

10. **Mithradates**, a male slave belonging to Games President Julius Spartiaticus.

11. Duovir **Acilius Candidus**. elected mayor for the current year 54/55 CE. A coin is being issued in his honor.

12. Duovir **Fulvius Flaccus**. Also elected for the current year 54/55 CE. A coin is also being issued in his honor. He is a wealthy banker from a family of businessmen with Roman roots.

13. **Sarapais**, a female slave of Junia Theodora, whose name suggests some past connection with the temple of Serapis in Alexandria, Egypt.

14. **Publius Regulus**, duovir in 50/51.

15. **Paconius Flaminus**, duovir in 50/51. He was a wealthy businessman from a business family active in Greece, with roots in Rome.

16. **Octavius Eucharistus**, duovir for two terms, 42/43 and 45/46.

17. **Licinius Priseus**, also duovir twice. His father was once the victor at an Isthmian Games race.

18. **Calendas**, a male slave.

19–29. If needed, additional participants can serve as male slaves, with names such as: Toxilus, Elpis, Epaphroditus, Sarapammon, Cerius, Seleneus, Eutachas, Isidoros, Europus, Hermas, Zonius, Matthias.

PREPARATION

The most critical role is that of Domitian Quadratus and may be assigned to a group leader. Let others be chosen by lot. If there are not enough actors for each role, have some play more than one part. Decorate your space to suggest elegance and privilege. Have an appropriate number of chairs arranged in a circle, with a seat for each slave to the left rear of his or her master. Make the Roman governor's seat appear especially elegant. On the wall place one or more portraits of the Caesars and a variety of inscriptions, such as:

"Caesar Claudius—We Hail You"
"To Divine Augustus—The Beginning of Life and Living"
"Hail to Caesar—Defender of Peace and Security"
"Hail World-Conquering Caesar, Son of God"
"Ave Caesar—Blessed Father of the Fatherland"
"Great is Artemis of the Ephesians"
"Great is Poseidon of the Corinthians"

Optional but recommended: ask participants to dress appropriately for their parts, in a flowing, toga-like garment with showy jewelry and bright sashes; but slaves need to dress very simply in drab colors and in short garments (so they can work!).

THE SIMULATION

Gathering of Corinthian Notables
Time: Spring, 54 CE, on the eve of Imperial Isthmian Games
Place: Banquet room of the Asclepieion, sanctuary of the healing god Asclepius

I. Seating of guests and opening words—games assistant
Domitian Quadratus
*Games coordinator Domitian Quadratus ushers in each
notable to their assigned place, with servants following
meekly behind. Last to enter, as all stand, is the Roman
governor. Domitian Quadratus, who is the facilitator,
then offers opening comments such as the following:*

> Welcome to the Imperial Isthmian and Caesarian
> Games. The gods have indeed been good to Corinth!
> In gratitude, the high priests of Asclepius, in whose
> banquet hall we recline, are even now offering a
> sacrifice of fruits and nuts to our awesome god of
> healing, Asclepius, for the health and well-being of all
> you dignitaries and civic leaders, and the athletes and
> artists competing in these Imperial Isthmian Games.
>
> Let us raise our voices in praise to the gods!

II. Hymn to the gods (*chanted*)—led by Domitian Quadratus

> Praise to Poseidon, great god of the seas.
> Bless Aphrodite, blessed giver of love.
> Hail great Apollo, first born of Zeus.
> Glory to Claudius, the son of god.

III. Official welcome—Julius Spartiaticus, agonothete/
president of the games

> Dear friends, I welcome you cordially. We are espe-
> cially graced by the presence of the Most Honorable
> Roman Governor of Greece. (*Bow to him.*) Having
> just arrived from Rome, he will make a special
> pronouncement at the end of our reception.
>
> What a very remarkable group of nobles you are! All
> of you are so wise by all human standards, you are
> powerful without question, you are mostly of noble
> birth and certainly all of noble rank. In their wisdom
> the gods have chosen us, the wise, to shame the fool-
> ish. The gods have chosen us who are strong to shame

the weak. The gods have chosen us, the mighty and respected, to rule over those who are nothing, lowly and despised. This is the meaning of leadership, is it not? And so when we boast, we boast with justifiable pride. [*Compare with 1 Corinthians 1–3.*]

I also would like to offer a very cordial welcome to our special guest, Junia Theodora, highly acclaimed head of the Lycian Embassy. (*Polite applause.*)

Inasmuch as we do not all know each other—and even those we know may have garnered new honors since last we met—I ask you to please introduce yourself, mentioning your civic offices, devotion to the gods, and recent benefactions.

IV. Introductions—games assistant Quadratus
Here each in turn seeks to impress as they boast about their offices, piety, and good deeds.

V. Boasting about cosmopolitan Corinth—Duovir Acilius Candidus

On behalf of the Corinthian government I want to boast about Corinth's cosmopolitan character. We're extremely proud to embrace so many unique peoples, so many religious expressions, so many varied ways of life from all across this vast empire. Over these last one hundred years we've embraced a steady stream of residents and colonists from Rome, Asia, Egypt, Syria, Judea, Africa, Italy, Crete, Macedonia—you name it—to create a city of virtually unparalleled genius, commerce, accomplishment and religious devotion. No matter what your origins or your favorite deity, you can rise as far as your talent and your wisdom can take you. Take, for example, the late Babbius Philinus of blessed memory, father of Babbius Italicus. Once upon a time he was a slave, yet made a stunning success of himself in business, held our highest offices, donated gorgeous buildings, and served as *pontifex*, chief priest of Neptune. As his son, Babbius Italicus, please take a bow!

VI. Reassurance about security—Duovir Fulvius Flaccus

Some of you have asked about the question of
security, so let me offer a word of reassurance. You
know that last month an official of our city was taken
hostage. The matter has been fully resolved; the city
official has been returned unharmed. The hostage-
taking may have been provoked by that unruly sect
of Jeshua followers, some party among the Jews.
Criminal activity, you know, often arises from these
unpatriotic atheists. Just as a precaution we have
beefed up security for this week and expanded our
random checks of suspicious-looking people who
might be brandishing knives and clubs. Rest assured,
the emperor's pledge of "peace and security" will be
upheld here in Corinth this week.

VII. Welcoming the new governor—Julius Spartiaticus, agonothete

I want to thank those of you from our stellar Isthmian
Games team of grand marshals. (*Have them stand.*)
They have put together an exceptionally fine tribute
to the great Caesar Augustus, divine savior of humanity, author of history, on whose birthday each year
begins, and to his latest successor, the most honorable, esteemed, and worthy son of god, the Emperor
Claudius.

Thus we welcome with extreme cordiality and highest
respect the imperial legate, the close personal friend of
the emperor, his lordship, Governor Atticus Antonius.
(*Applause as he is crowned with a wreath.*)

At the close of the games, his lordship will bestow
special honors on certain individuals who have won
the emperor's favor: land grants, tax exemptions, and
business licenses. We Corinthians are hoping and praying for imperial sponsorship of the long awaited canal
across the narrows of the isthmus. As your lordship
knows, goods now must either be valiantly carried

across the isthmus from one ship to another. Nothing could enhance our prosperity more than realizing this dream of over seven centuries. Such a magnificent public work would be a signature accomplishment of Emperor Claudius's long and illustrious reign.

VIII. Pledge of Allegiance to the image of Caesar—led by Publius Regulus

In honor of our new governor, let us recite our Pledge of Allegiance. (*Face the image of Caesar*)

"I pledge allegiance to the imperial image
and to the Empire of Rome for which it stands,
one empire, ordained by the gods, indivisible,
with peace and security for all."

IX. A pitch for Corinth—Grand Marshal Ventidius Fronto

Let me add that digging the canal could not come at a more opportune time. Notwithstanding the present grain shortages the masses complain about, prosperity abounds as never before. Goods are piled high on both sides of the isthmus, awaiting movement to ships on the opposite side. We could not be in a more commercially strategic location. Our own products have a wide reputation, especially those of copper and bronze. There is no more famous commercial moniker than "Corinthian bronze." Thank you, Claudius Optatus! And we have never looked better. The newest addition to our stunning Roman-style architecture is the most glorious new shrine to Venus, mother of the Roman nation.

X. Comments by guests—Games Assistant Quadratus

Would any of you guests care to offer a word at this time?

Here some should complain about not being seated close to and on the right of the Roman governor or about their accommodations, food, or charioteers. Those happy with

*their seats and other hospitality should offer words meant
to impress the Roman governor.*

XI. Preview of daily events—Games Assistant Quadratus,
grand marshals
*The games assistant announces that the preview of events
for the games will be in the form of a rhetorical competition. Each grand marshal has up to four minutes to
announce the activities he has scheduled for his day. The
winner will be chosen by vote of all present (except slaves,
of course, and the governor, who votes only in case of a
tie).*

XII. Awarding of golden grain to the winner—Governor
Atticus Antonius
*The governor offers appropriate praise and suggests the
winner may receive special favors from the emperor.*

XIII. About our religious devotion—Grand Marshal
Claudius Optatus

> I need not remind you of the importance of leading
> the people in piety. We are known by our devotion
> to the gods and to the divinized Caesar Augustus,
> and the splendid succession of divinity wearing of the
> imperial purple. Their praise is offered everywhere.
> Look at these very walls. Let us together stand and
> shout out these praises. (*Everyone shouts them out
> together.*) And would you remain standing as we
> make our confession of faith, led by our retiring
> *pontifex.*

XIV. Confession of Faith—led by Pontifex Julius Polyaenus
[*This is an authentic Roman pledge*]

> I swear by Zeus, the earth, the sun,
> and by all the gods and goddesses, including Augustus
> himself,
> to be favorable to Caesar Augustus, his sons and
> descendants forever,
> in speech, in actions, and in thoughts,

considering as friends those he considers so,
and regarding as enemies those he judges so.
And to defend their interests I will spare
neither body, nor soul, nor life, nor my children . . .

The rites of homage and sacrifice constitute a constant
feature of our common life. No day goes by without
multiple sacrifices in Corinth to the gods and to the
imperial authority. To find an atheist in Corinth
would take you a full day's investigation! Yes, we
have a few Jews and other atheists who reject the gods
and the divinity of the imperial line, just as in any
large city, but they are without influence and likely on
the decrease. Such atheism implies a lack of patriotism
that we must, over time, eradicate from our midst.

XV. Contest to choose an inscription—Games Assistant
Quadratus [*optional*]
Before the contest begins, have all present stand and again
shout out each of the inscriptions on the walls, which
serve as examples for what follows. Quadratus explains
that the governor has asked for this competition to create
an appropriate marble inscription for a new esplanade.

Each one present is to propose an inscription to be
placed prominently along the esplanade, which is being
donated by a foreign dignitary. It may be up to nine
words long and should incorporate adulation for Caesar
and/or a god. Five minutes will be allowed for each noble
to compose their proposed inscription. They may receive
the help of any slave with them. Each proposed inscrip-
tion should be written out and placed on the wall. The
governor makes the decision and awards a special sash or
trophy to the winner.

XVI. Announcements and concerns—Games Assistant
Quadratus [*optional*]
At this time the slaves are dismissed to fetch the (optional)
surprise treat and glasses of water for a toast, and Quadratus
invites the duoviri to make their pronouncements.

Duovir Fulvius Flaccus announces that because of the
unrest regarding the serious grain shortage, the duoviri are

appointing a grain master with broad powers to address the shortage and that that person is Claudius Dinippus, an experienced leader who has performed this important task on two previous occasions.

XVII. Surprise treat—Agonothete Julius Spartiaticus [*optional*]
Spartiaticus explains the special treat he has arranged and how privileged we are to partake of the very nuts, grains, and fruits just sacrificed earlier this evening to the god Asclepius. Just for fun, the treat might be called a "Caesar Salad."

XVIII. Any more concerns?—Games Assistant Domitian Quadratus [*optional*]

XIX. Concluding remarks—Roman Governor Atticus Antonius

> And now before we depart and get a good night's rest for the exciting week ahead—the big pronouncement. I have just returned from Rome with some great news for Corinth and all of Achaia. The request of the cities to inaugurate a province-wide celebration of the Imperial Julio-Claudio Dynasty has been approved, to begin with the accession of the next emperor. (*applause*) And the host city is, I am delighted to announce, Corinth itself! (*more applause*) We wish Emperor Claudius many more years, but he's not been well of late and we want to be prepared.
>
> Finally, I want to announce that, for this new provincial observance, I have chosen as the high priest for life, the *pontifex maximus*, none other than this year's Isthmian Games president, Julius Spartiaticus. No one is more deserving. Congratulations, Mr. President! (*applause*)

XX. Closing benediction/toast—Julius Spartiaticus, games president/agonothete

Thank you so much. I am overwhelmed by your trust.
May Jupiter, Venus, Neptune and the divinized imperial family be truly honored by all we do.

In conclusion, let me remind you of the famous
proverb everyone knows well: "Not for everyone is
a voyage to Corinth." That is, Corinth is not for the
faint of heart. We strive hard here; we play hard; we
compete intensely in commerce, in public life, even
in love. Like the runners and wrestlers, we give our
all. And when we win, we win big. It's every man for
himself, but the rewards are worth it. As in a popular
song here in Corinth: "If you can make it here, you'll
make it anywhere!"

You have made it here in Corinth—and this puts
you in a special category of the brave-hearted, the
adventurous, the lovers of sport and competition, the
true lovers of life. Welcome to the Imperial Isthmian
Games! Let us together offer a closing toast. (*Hands
or glasses are raised.*)

May all the blessings of victory, prosperity, glory,
peace, and security rest upon Mother Rome, chosen
ruler of the world. And may every blessing rest upon
Emperor Claudius, son of god and author of all good
things. In the name of the divine Caesars and the gods
who dwell forever on Mount Olympus, Amen!

APPENDIX 2

LEADER'S GUIDE

GETTING STARTED

First review the introduction to this book. Then read the following guidelines, which are especially applicable to a church or study group. For an academic setting, also see the website www.HeraldPress.com/CreatingAScene.

Publicity. Most people in your group may not be familiar with biblical simulation. We recommend publicizing this study several weeks ahead of time. Use consecutive notices in your church bulletin, on the church website, or through email. Create snatches of conversation from an imagined debate in Chloe's house church to tease and attract participants. The sample announcement in the web supplement (www.HeraldPress.com/CreatingAScene) was performed in one congregation at the end of a worship service two weeks ahead of time and attracted twenty-five participants.

Time commitment. Regular attendance throughout the study is important for two reasons: (1) each person plays a particular character in the house church and is needed for the total functioning of the group; (2) the experience in each session builds on the previous one.

For a setting with irregular attendance the simulation can work as long as two or three representatives are present from each faction. After all, illness or the demands of slavery must have also affected attendance in ancient

Corinth. A visitor to the group may play the role of an interested Corinthian citizen or a curious traveler or sailor from one of Corinth's ports. (See "A Visitor's Guide to Corinth" in web supplement at www.HeraldPress.com/CreatingAScene.)

The ideal time frame is twelve or thirteen sessions of two hours each. However, this is often unrealistic and can be adjusted. The role-play itself does not begin until chapter 8, so chapters 1–7 can be read outside of the session. The first two or three sessions, then, can be used for clarifying questions, organizing house church groups, and developing characters.

Size of group. You will need ten to twenty-five participants, divided into four factions. See "Extra Material for Character Development in Corinth" in web supplement for more than eighteen characters.

Don't just read—perform! Either the leader or a skilled reader should read aloud each section of Paul's letter to the house church. Phoebe is a natural choice since she is the "minister" (*diakonos*) of the house church in the nearby port town of Cenchreae (Romans 16:1-2), and we have designated her as a cousin and friend of Chloe's, who leads one house church in the city of Corinth. As a coworker with Paul, Phoebe understands him and is able to read and interpret his letter to all the local house churches. If the group is small, Chloe could be both reader and house church leader.

However, if a man is leader, he can be Stephanas, leader of a different house church, but the one who has taken the Corinthians' letter to Paul and brought back his response (1 Corinthians 16:17; see chapter 1). As an educated man, he is able to read and interpret Paul's letter.

Each reading should be a performance. We have condensed and paraphrased the text so it can be read conversationally, as if Paul were directly speaking to your group. The section headings you see in some readings are not to be read out loud; they are there to help navigation and break up the page. No sing-song or monotone Scripture reading that tunes out the listeners! When something seems specifically directed towards one faction or one class of persons (such as slaves or patrons), the reader should specifically address that group.

Note: The audience should be paying attention to the reader and not following along in the Bible or this book. Few people in Chloe's house church could read, and *no one* would have had a copy of Paul's letter at this time!

Be sure to have:

- A copy of this book for each participant

- A Bible for each participant (recommended)

- Reusable name tags (plastic with paper insert); use a different color for each faction

- Felt tip markers

- A small bell to ring for beginning and ending role-playing in the Corinthian house church (optional)

- A safe place (box or bag) in which to keep name tags, markers, bell, etc.

- Refreshments (optional, but nice for a longer evening session); use foods eaten in the Middle East—grape juice, wheat crackers, raisins, hummus, pita bread, nuts, or dates (see recipes in chapter 18)

BACKGROUND SESSIONS: WE REIMAGINE CORINTH AND ESTABLISH A HOUSE CHURCH

The first eight chapters of this book contain necessary orientation for re-creating our house church. The number and length of sessions for setting up the simulation depends on time constraints and the maturity, advance knowledge, and preparation of participants. You may save time by asking participants to read chapters 1 and 3 *before* the first session. Supposing each session lasts for one hour, we recommend the following:

Session one
Objective: to visualize the cultural and geographical context.
Equipment: Internet access, projector and screen

Show the PowerPoint introduction, "A Visit to Ancient Corinth" (download it at www.HeraldPress. com/CreatingAScene). We as coauthors have visited Corinth and its surroundings, accompanied by Dr. David Pettegrew, an archeologist who does ongoing research at Corinth.[1] Each photo is annotated. There are also additional slides at the end (*optional*) that illustrate how one group presented their study of 1 Corinthians in a worship service, followed by the Lord's Supper in the context of an *agape* meal.

If there is time, and if participants have read at least chapter 1, discuss these questions:

1. How does this sociohistorical simulation approach differ from other ways you have learned about Paul's letters?
2. If you read chapter 3, what questions do you have about why Paul wrote 1 Corinthians? Encourage the group to read chapters 1 and 3 if they have not already read them.

Session two (or the second hour of a two-hour session)
Objective: to further contextualize Paul's letter through a virtual walking tour of Corinth.
Equipment: same as for session one.

A slide show, "Time Traveling," is available online at www.HeraldPress.com/CreatingAScene, to be used in conjunction with the chapter. Notations throughout the chapter show where each slide fits in.

Use chapter 2 as a readers theatre portraying geographical orientation and Roman-Corinthian customs, with group members assigned to be different characters. Since Babbius Italicus (a historical first-century Corinthian) has

---

1. David Pettegrew teaches Roman history at Messiah College, Grantham, Pa. See his website at www.corinthianmatters.com.

the most lines, you might choose three different participants to share this part. Assign chapters 5 and 6 for the
next session (include chapters 1 and 4 if the group has
not already read them). If you have a two-hour session,
include reading chapters 7 and 8 and begin setting up factions and choosing characters.

Alternative for session two

Replace chapter 2 with appendix 1: "Arrogant
Aristocrats in Action." This role-play portrays a reception for the aristocrats in Corinth the evening before the
Panhellenic Games begin in the spring of 54 CE. The
struggle for power and superiority display the dominant
cultural values in contrast to those expressed or implied
in Paul's letter of 1 Corinthians.

Having everyone dress for their part makes for a compelling experience. Flowing garments for the nobles, with
colorful sashes and gaudy jewelry works well; drab colors, no jewelry, and knee-length garments are appropriate
for slaves. When everyone joins in, people soon get over
their initial discomfort and feel liberated to portray their
character. Participants experience different sides of themselves and come away with an understanding of the elite
Corinthian ethos that is virtually unforgettable. Let roles
be chosen by lot, so no favoritism is shown. Let the Fates
decide!

This role-play requires at least eight to ten characters.
For fewer participants or a shorter time period, reciting
several speeches and the unison parts can still give the
flavor of imperial religion and the struggle for power
and honor. An abbreviated experience can be done in
ten minutes or so and would require three speakers, with
everyone joining in for the unison parts. The abbreviated
version would include these sections from appendix 1.

    I.   Opening words

    II.   Hymn to the gods (in unison)

    III. Official welcome

    VIII. Pledge of Allegiance to the image of
              Caesar (in unison)

XIV. Confession of Faith (in unison)

XX. Closing words, benediction, and toast (the latter in unison)

Session three
Objectives:

- To discuss assigned chapters, including the concept of hidden messages in Paul's letters discussed in our chapter 4

- To get each participant into a faction

- To choose character roles and create nametags

After discussing the assigned chapters, the main task is to divide into factions where members choose character roles according to chapter 5. One method is to number off by fours and designate each number for one faction. However, it is important that the Apollos faction comprises more *males*, and the Christ faction more *females*. Thus, early in this process the leader may have to intervene and ask some participants to exchange factions. For smaller groups or younger participants, the leader may want to assign particular roles.

Send each faction to a different corner of the room to decide who plays which role, using the material in chapter 5. If there are fewer than eighteen participants, make sure that characters are chosen in the order in which they are listed so that the size of the factions will be more or less equal.

Hand out and create nametags for each faction, each with a different color. If desired, have members note something relevant to help others make connections, i.e., occupation, "wife/husband of ___," "slave of ___," etc.

Assign chapters 6 and 7. Be sure to collect nametags at end of each session!

Session four
Objectives:

- To discuss issues from previous chapters, including social class and religious backgrounds in chapters 6 and 8

- To clarify social backgrounds of each of the factions and the tensions they have with each other

- To have each member of Chloe's house church introduce him/herself to the total group

Have participants sit in a circle, but beside members of their own faction for solidarity. Emphasize in the discussion how crucial these chapters are because they deal with hierarchy and social status—and the ways lower-class people resist those of higher status. Much of Paul's advice in his letter deals with the gospel's challenge to bring together into one body people from widely different social classes who are faithful to God's countercultural reign.

Clarify the social backgrounds of each of these factions and how they may be relating to each other as they listen to Paul's letter. Who has extra privileges, and what are they? Who is a slave—and (possibly) to which patron or owner in the group? How does each person's role represent their faction and their social status? Who pulls rank over whom? How might slaves resist their status? How faithful, or not, is each to resisting the imperial religion and values?

Allow time for each faction to meet together and further flesh out their characters in light of chapters 6 and 7. Then gather again and ask each group member to briefly introduce themselves to the larger house church. Who is related to whom? Who is patron to whom? Who is a slave to which master? How did you come to believe?

Assign chapter 8 for the next session. Ask the woman playing Chloe to prepare ahead of time to briefly introduce Phoebe (or Stephanas) to the group. She can use some of the description of Phoebe from chapter 7. If the reader is Stephanas, she can draw from his description in chapter 1 and 1 Corinthians 16:17.

THE PLAY BEGINS! REENACTING CHLOE'S HOUSE CHURCH

Session five—1 Corinthians 1:1-9
Objectives:

- To understand Greco-Roman letter writing and the importance of rhetoric as persuasive speech

- To introduce Phoebe (or Stephanas) as the

reader/performer of 1 Corinthians

- To begin the actual simulation of Chloe's house church hearing Paul's letter

- To analyze Paul's greetings and thanksgiving (1 Corinthians 1:1-9) in light of Greco-Roman letters and persuasive techniques, as well as the hidden message in speaking of "the Lord Jesus Christ"

Reserve time for three "acts." Once the simulation begins, think in terms of three parts to each session:

- Act 1— Preparation. Discuss the assigned chapter, including questions about characters, factions, and their interrelationships.

- Act 2—Reenact Chloe's house church. This includes reading/performing the text for that session plus the responses to the reading among the characters and factions.

- Act 3—Make connections. Participants use questions at the end of each chapter to reflect on how this part of Paul's message can speak to believers today.

For a one-hour session, plan for (Act 1) 15 minutes; (Act 2) 30 minutes; (Act 3) 15 minutes. However, time for preparation may lessen in later simulations as participants get used to the role-play.

For a forty-five-minute weekly session, plan for (Act 1) 10 minutes; (Act 2) 25 minutes; (Act 3) 10 minutes. The group will probably feel under time pressure, and the discussion on contemporary connections will be short-changed. One option is to alternate sessions at this point. The first session is for preparation and role-play, and the following session is to discuss the text's meaning for today. In that case, only half of the chapters can be used, or the study can be stretched into more sessions.

Getting in gear. Make sure everyone has a nametag, this book, and a Bible. Members sit according to their faction but in one large group. Ask if there are questions related to "Understanding the background" in chapter 8. Stress that, when the bell rings, everyone assumes their role throughout Phoebe's introduction, the reading of the text, and the house church discussion. After the bell rings again, they can move back into the present to discuss and analyze the simulation, their own roles, and the interpretation of the text for today.

Reassure the participants that each character is important to the discussion, no matter how outrageous her or his opinions. Extreme opinions *should* be put forth, so that as the study proceeds, some might be convinced, convicted, or at least tempered by hearing Paul's arguments. Paul's letter was not authoritative Scripture at that time. To some believers, Apollos or Cephas (Peter) was more amenable to their background or lifestyle. The charismatic, woman-affirming Christ-faction in particular may think they have gone beyond Paul in their exercise of freedom in the Spirit. See further instructions under the heading "Preparing for the simulation" in chapter 8.

Introduction of Phoebe (or Stephanas) reading the text. Ask Chloe to introduce the oral reader after you ring the bell. After personal greetings, the reader acknowledges the introduction and proceeds to read 1 Corinthians 1:1-9. Remind the group to *listen* very closely and try to remember what they hear.

House church discussion. Because we do not remember what we hear orally as well as nonreaders do, we now make an exception and use the biblical text to make sure we heard correctly. Use the questions under the heading, "Responding to Paul's letter as a house church" in chapter 8. Either the leader (Phoebe or Stephanas) or Chloe can facilitate this. Expect some awkwardness for the first time!

Debriefing and applying. Ring the bell so there are ten to thirty minutes at the end of the hour (or two) for this essential aspect of our study. Use the "Debriefing and applying" questions at the end of chapter 8.

For this first session, probably more time than later

will be spent analyzing the reenactment, since this is a new experience. However, as people get used to role-playing, later sessions should move quickly into reflection on how to connect Paul's message to our current lives and situations. That is the goal and primary purpose for studying 1 Corinthians. Applications are not always easy to make; it will be the leader's job to continually stress this connection.

Assign 1 Corinthians 1:10–3:4 and chapter 9 of this book for the next session.

Sessions six through thirteen or fourteen (chapters 9–17)
The structure of all of these sessions will be similar to session five, except for Phoebe's introduction. Use a few minutes to get organized and make sure all participants have their nametags and other materials and know the roles they are playing. Take time to stress the main ideas from "Understanding the background" of the relevant chapter, and encourage questions from participants that cannot be dealt with during the role-play.

Then proceed to the simulation, with Phoebe (or another reader) reading the text, followed by responses from all factions of the house church. Ring the bell to allow time to debrief and discuss contemporary applications of Paul's message.

Assign the appropriate chapter to read before the next session.

Note: If you are limited to thirteen sessions (as in a Sunday school quarter), we would recommend combining material from chapters 9 and 10—or eliminating chapter 10. First Corinthians 1:10–4:21 is a unified section making the theological case for unity in the church. If you decide to combine parts of 1:10–4:21, then retain texts that relate most to the flow of the argument. For the discussion, focus primarily on material in chapter 9.

Last session—chapter 18
The final session is an *agape* meal modeled on the Corinthian "Supper of the Lord" (11:17-34 and 14:26-33a). This experience brings closure to the simulation. Participants can bring something from the recipe collection. Encourage them to bring family members or other

interested friends. Use the outline in chapter 18 for the meal and worship experience. This may be held at a different time if convenient. For example, follow the last session in Sunday school with a Corinthian meal over the noon hour.

VARIATIONS AND ADAPTATIONS

What can you do with fewer sessions? In all cases, it is helpful to have participants receive a copy of the book beforehand and read at least chapters 1 and 3. Encourage them to read all the background chapters on their own to enrich the simulation. The *agape* meal may be an extra session, or an extension of the last session.

- *Ten sessions*: Use readers theater of chapter 2, along with accompanying PowerPoint slides in the first session. Depending on length of sessions, include the ten-minute performance of appendix 1. Allow two more sessions to get Chloe's house church organized. Omit role-playing 1 Corinthians 8 and 10 (chapter 13), and choose between including chapter 12 or chapter 14, depending on the interests or needs of the group.

- *Eight sessions*: Retain first three sessions as above. Role-play chapters 9, 11, 13, 15, and 17. If spiritual gifts of chapter 16 are an important topic for your group, substitute that in place of another chapter.

- *Six sessions*: Depending on length of the sessions, the first one can include (1) some slides from the main PowerPoint presentation; or (2) chapter 2 with PowerPoint slides. After a short introduction, move to the factions and character roles in chapter 5. Get everyone into a faction and, if possible, have each one choose a character. For the second session, take time to meet as factions and further develop characters. Discuss why Paul wrote this letter (chapter 3) and patronage and slavery (chapter 6). For the following four sessions, choose four chapters to simulate, prefer-

ably from chapters 9, 11, 13, 15, 16, 17, or 18.
If these are two-hour sessions, a different chapter
may be role-played in each hour.

- *Five sessions, as for an overnight retreat*: Have
  participants read as much as possible of chapters
  3 through 7. In the first session do the readers
  theater (chapter 2) and begin discussion of the
  introductory chapters, emphasizing the hidden
  messages of resistance, imperial religion, and
  social class. In session two, do the full or abbreviated version of the simulation in appendix 1
  (see above) and have participants choose characters for the house church factions (chapter 5). In
  session three do chapter 8 of our text; in session
  four, do a combination of chapters 14 and 15.
  Then in session five close the experience with the
  agape meal of chapter 18.

- *Two sessions*: For the first session, either show
  main PowerPoint visual introduction to Corinth
  or use the readers theater in chapter 2, along
  with the PowerPoint slides that coordinate with
  it. Use the following instructions from "One session" below. Use whatever time is left in the first
  session to explain the simulation method and the
  emphasis on social class and resistance to Roman
  ways in 1 Corinthians. The second session can
  proceed as described below.

- *One session*: focus on chapter 15—1 Corinthians
  11:17-34.

  o If you have only one hour (such as on Sunday
    morning), first explain (1) the simulation
    method; (2) imperial religion and Roman
    Domination versus the Jesus Movement; (3)
    the emphasis on social class in 1 Corinthians
    and how strongly Paul feels that those with
    privilege should share it or give it up for the
    sake of the unity of the body.

o Ask someone to read about the four factions in 1 Corinthians 1:11-12.

o Number off from one to four, telling participants to make sure there is a majority of men in group 1 ("those of Apollos") and a majority of women in group 4 ("those of Christ"). Have each faction sit together—if possible in a large circle in one corner of the room.

o Read a paragraph from a representative character from each of the factions (see "Extra Material for Character Development in Corinth" in the web supplement at www .HeraldPress.com/CreatingAScene). Tell them there are complaints from the working classes and slaves against the Apollos group, who are the wealthier and more educated patrons. They share a meal together in the late afternoon. Thus, most of the food is gone by the time the workers arrive. What should be done?

o Use remaining time to make contemporary connections. If more time is needed, and there is opportunity the following week for more discussion, use it!

BIBLIOGRAPHY

Ancient Sources

Apuleius. *The Golden Ass 11.24.6–25.6.*

Juvenal: The Sixteen Satires. Trans. Peter Green. Penguin Classics. New York: Penguin Books, 1967.

Origen. *Against Celsus.*

Plutarch. *Moralia 140B*, "Advice to the Bride and Groom."

Secondary Sources

Avery, Richard, and Donald Marsh. "We Are the Church." Words and music, Carol Stream, IL: Hope Publishing Co., 1972.

Bagnell, Roger S. "Missing Females in Roman Egypt." Scripta Classica Israelica 16 (1997): 121–38.

Balch, David L., ed. *Homosexuality, Science, and the "Plain Sense" of Scripture.* Grand Rapids, MI: Eerdmans, 2000.

———. "Two Roman Colonies: Pompeii and Corinth." Paper presented at the annual meeting of the Society of Biblical Literature, Atlanta, GA, November 21, 2010.

Barlett, Donald L. and James B. Steele, *The Betrayal of the American Dream.* New York: Perseus Books, 2012.

Barr, David L. *New Testament Story: An Introduction.* 4th edition. Belmont, CA: Wadsworth/Thomson Learning, 2009.

Bassler, Jouette M. "First Corinthians and Community Disagreements." Pages 23–34 in J. Shannon Clarkson, ed., *Conflict and Community in the Corinthian Church.*

New York: Women's Division, General Board of Global Ministries, The United Methodist Church, 2000.

Bell, John L. "So Much Wrong." *Sing the Story: Hymnal: A Worship Book—Supplement 2*. Scottdale, PA: Faith & Life Resources, 2007.

——— and Graham Maule. "If the War Goes On." *Sing the Journey: Hymnal: A Worship Book—Supplement 1*. Scottdale, PA: Faith & Life Resources, 2005.

Bishop, Jim. "Gathering Explores Anabaptist Message in Visual Age." *Mennonite Weekly Review*. November 7, 2011, 12.

Borg, Marcus J., and John Dominic Crossan. *The First Paul: Reclaiming the Radical Visionary Behind the Church's Conservative Icon*. New York, NY: HarperOne, 2009.

———. *The Last Week: What the Gospels Really Teach about Jesus's Final Days in Jerusalem*. San Francisco, CA: HarperCollins, 2006.

Bradley, Keith R. "On the Roman Slave Supply and Slavebreeding." Pages 42–64 in *Classical Slavery*. Edited by M. I. Finley. London: Frank Cass & Co., 1987.

Burkert, Walter. *Ancient Mystery Cults*. Cambridge, MS: Harvard University Press, 1987.

Carney, Thomas Francis. *The Shape of the Past: Models and Antiquity*. Lawrence, KS: Coronado Press, 1975.

Carter, Warren. *The Roman Empire and the New Testament: An Essential Guide*. Nashville, TN: Abingdon, 2006.

Cary, M., and H. H. Scullard, *A History of Rome Down to the Reign of Constantine*. London: Macmillan, 1975.

Chow, John K. *Patronage and Power: A Study of Social Networks in Corinth*. JSNT, sup 7. Sheffield: JSOT, 1992.

Cooney, Rory. "My Soul Cries Out." *Sing the Journey: Hymnal: A Worship Book—Supplement 1*. Scottdale, PA: Faith & Life Resources, 2005.

Cosby, Michael. *Apostle on the Edge: An Inductive Approach to Paul*. Louisville, KY: Westminster/John Knox, 2009.

Crossan, John Dominic. *God and Empire: Jesus against Rome, Then and Now*. San Francisco, CA: HarperSanFrancisco, 2007.

Crossan, John Dominic, and Jonathan L. Reed. *In Search of Paul: How Jesus's Apostle Opposed Rome's Empire with God's Kingdom*. San Francisco: HarperCollins, 2004.

D'Arms, J. H. "The Roman Convivium and the Idea of Equality." Pages 303–20 in *Sympotica: A Symposium on the Symposion*. Edited by O. Murray. Oxford: Oxford University Press, 1990.

Day, Nancy. *Your Travel Guide to Ancient Greece*. Minneapolis, MN: Runestone Press, 2001.

Daw, Carl P., Jr. "Till All the Jails Are Empty." *Common Ground: A Song Book for All the Churches*. Edinburgh: Saint Andrew Press, 1998.

Elliott, Neil. "The Apostle Paul and Empire." Pages 97–116 in *In the Shadow of Empire: Reclaiming the Bible as a History of Faithful Resistance*. Edited by Richard A. Horsley. Louisville, KY: Westminster/ JohnKnox, 2008.

———. *The Arrogance of Nations: Reading Romans in the Shadow of the Empire*. Minneapolis, MN: Fortress Press, 2008.

Engels, Donald. *Roman Corinth: An Alternate Model for the Classical City*. Chicago: University of Chicago Press, 1990.

Farrell, Bernadette. "God Has Chosen Me." *Sing the Story: Hymnal: A Worship Book—Supplement 2*. Scottdale, PA: Faith & Life Resources, 2007.

Ferguson, John. *The Religions of the Roman Empire*. Ithaca, NY: Cornell University Press, 1970.

Finger, Reta Halteman. *Paul and the Roman House Churches: a Simulation*. Scottdale, PA: Herald Press, 1993.

———. *Roman House Churches for Today: A Practical Guide for Small Groups*, 2nd edition. Grand Rapids, MI: Eerdmans, 2007. [A reissue of *Paul and the Roman House Churches*.]

———. *Of Widows and Meals: Communal Meals in the Book of Acts*. Grand Rapids, MI: Eerdmans, 2007.

Fosdick, Harry Emerson. "God of Grace and God of Glory." *The United Methodist Hymnal*. Nashville, TN: The United Methodist Publishing House, 1989.

Franke, Bob. "Alleluia, the Great Storm is Over." *Sing the Journey: Hymnal: A Worship Book—Supplement 1.* Scottdale, PA: Faith & Life Resources, 2005.

Fredrickson, David E. "Natural and Unnatural Use in Romans 1:24-27: Paul and the Philosophic Critique of Eros." Pages 197–222 in *Homosexuality, Science, and the "Plain Sense"of Scripture.* Edited by David L. Balch. Grand Rapids, MI: Eerdmans, 2000.

Friesen, Steven J. "The Wrong Erastus: Ideology, Archaeology, and Exegesis." Pages 231–56 in *Corinth in Context: Comparative Studies on Religion and Society.* Edited by Steven J. Friesen, Daniel N. Schowalter, and James C. Walters. Leiden, Netherlands: Brill, 2010.

Futrell, Alison. *The Roman Games.* Malden, MS: Blackwell Publishing, 2006.

Gaeade, Beth Ann, ed. *Congregations Talking about Homosexuality.* Herndon, VA: Alban Institute, 1998.

Galloway, Kathy. "Sing for God's Glory." *Common Ground: A Song Book for All the Churches.* Edinburgh: Saint Andrew Press, 1998.

Gillette, Carolyn Winfrey. *Gifts of Love: New Hymns for Today's Worship.* Louisville, KY: Geneva Press, 2000.

Glancy, Jennifer A. *Slavery in Early Christianity.* New York: Oxford University Press, 2002.

Goodman, Martin. *The Roman World: 44 BC–AD 180.* London, New York: Routledge, 1997.

Harrill, J. Albert. "Paul and Slavery." Pages 575–607 in *Paul in the Greco-Roman World.* Edited by J. Paul Sampley. Harrisburg, PA: Trinity Press International, 2003.

Hays, Richard B. *1 Corinthians.* Interpretation: A Bible Commentary for Teaching and Preaching. Louisville, KY: John Knox Press, 1997.

Heen, Erik M. "Phil 2:6-11 and Resistance to Local Timocratic Rule." Pages 125–53 in *Paul and the Roman Imperial Order.* Edited by Richard A. Horsley. Harrisburg, PA: Trinity Press, 2004.

Henderson, Suzanne Watts. "'If Anyone Hungers...': An Integrated Reading of 1 Cor. 11:17-34." *New Testament Studies* 48 (2002): 195–208.

Horsley, Richard. *1 Corinthians.* Nashville, TN: Abingdon Press, 1998.

———. "Rhetoric and Empire—and 1 Corinthians." Pages 72–102 in *Paul and Politics: Ekklesia, Israel, Imperium, Interpretation.* Edited by Richard Horsley. Harrisburg, PA: Trinity Press, 2000.

———. *Covenant Economics: A Biblical Vision of Justice for All.* Louisville, KY: Westminster/John Knox Press, 2009.

Horsley, Richard, ed. *Paul and Empire: Religion and Power in Roman Imperial Society.* Harrisburg, PA: Trinity Press, 1997.

———, ed. *Paul and Politics: Ekklesia, Israel, Imperium, Interpretation.* Harrisburg, PA: Trinity Press, 2000.

———, ed. *Paul and the Roman Imperial Order.* Harrisburg, PA: Trinity Press, 2004.

———, ed. *In the Shadow of Empire: Reclaiming the Bible as a History of Faithful Resistance.* Louisville, KY: Westminster/JohnKnox Press, 2008.

Huber, Jane Parker. *A Singing Faith.* Philadelphia, PA: The Westminster Press, 1987.

Jewett, Robert. "The Social Context and Implications of Homoerotic References in Romans 1:24-27." Pages 223–40 in *Homosexuality, Science, and the "Plain Sense" of Scripture.* Edited by David L. Balch. Grand Rapids, MI: Eerdmans, 2000.

Johnson, David W., Roger T. Johnson, and Karl A. Smith. "Constructive Controversy: The Educative Power of Intellectual Conflict." *Change* 1 (2000): 29–37.

Kaufman, Cathy. *Cooking in Ancient Civilizations.* Westport, CT: Greenwood Press, 2006.

Keener, Craig. S. *Paul, Women, and Wives: Marriage and Women's Ministry in the Letters of Paul.* Peabody, MA: Hendrickson, 1992.

Kennedy, George. *New Testament Interpretation through Rhetorical Criticism.* Chapel Hill and London: University of North Carolina Press, 1984.

Kendrick, Graham. "Beauty for Brokenness." *Sing the Story: Hymnal: A Worship Book—Supplement 2.* Scottdale, PA: Faith & Life Resources, 2007.

Kraemer, Ross S. *Her Share of the Blessings: Women's Religions among Pagans, Jews, and Christians in the Greco-Roman World.* New York, Oxford: Oxford University Press, 1993.

Laqueur, Thomas. *Making Sex: Body and Gender from the Greeks to Freud.* Cambridge, MA: Harvard University Press, 1990.

Lowenthal, David. *The Past Is a Foreign Country.* Cambridge: Cambridge University Press, 1985.

Lull, David and William Beardslee. *1 Corinthians.* Chalice Commentaries for Today. St. Louis, MO: Chalice Press, 2007.

Luscombe, Belinda. "Who Needs Marriage? A Changing Institution." *Time* (Nov 18, 2010). www.time.com/time/nation/article/0,8599,2031962-4,00.html.

MacMullen, Ramsay. *Roman Social Relations: 50 B.C. to A.D. 284.* New Haven, CT: Yale University Press, 1974.

Mann, Michael. *The Sources of Social Power: Vol. 1, A History of Power from the Beginning to AD 1760.* Cambridge: Cambridge University Press, 1986.

Martin, Dale. *The Corinthian Body.* New Haven, CT: Yale University Press, 1995.

Mitchell, Margaret M. *Paul and the Rhetoric of Reconciliation: An Exegetical Investigation of the Language and Composition of 1 Corinthians.* Louisville, KY: Westminster/JohnKnox Press, 1991.

Murphy-O'Connor, Jerome. *St. Paul's Corinth: Texts and Archeology.* 3rd edition. Collegeville, MN: The Liturgical Press, 2002.

Murray, Shirley Erena. "God of the Bible." *Sing the Journey: Hymnal: A Worship Book—Supplement 1.* Scottdale, PA: Faith & Life Resources, 2005.

———. "Touch the Earth Lightly." *Worship and Song.* Nashville, TN: Abingdon Press, 2011.

Okland, Jorumn. "Ceres, Kore, and Cultural Complexity: Divine Personality Definitions and Human Worshippers in Roman Corinth." Pages 199–229 in *Corinth in Context: Comparative Studies on Religion and Society.* Edited by Steven J. Friesen, Daniel N. Schowalter, and James C. Walters. Leiden, Netherlands: Brill, 2010.

Osiek, Carolyn, and Margaret Y. MacDonald. *A Woman's Place: House Churches in Earliest Christianity.* Minneapolis, MN: Fortress Press, 2006.

Patterson, Orlando. *Slavery and Social Death: A Comparative Study*. Cambridge: Harvard University Press, 1982.

Potter, David Stone, and David J. Mattingly, eds. *Life, Death, and Entertainment in the Roman Empire*. Ann Arbor, MI: University of Michigan Press, 2005.

Ramsaran, Rollin A. "Resisting Imperial Domination and Influence: Paul's Apocalyptic Rhetoric in 1 Corinthians." Pages 89–101 in *Paul and the Roman Imperial Order*. Edited by Richard Horsley. Harrisburg, MA: Trinity Press International, 2004.

Rivlin, Gary. "The Billion-Dollar Bank Heist." *Newsweek*, July 18, 2011.

Rohrbaugh, Richard. "The Pre-Industrial City in Luke-Acts: Urban Industrial Relations." Pages 125–49 in *The Social World of Luke-Acts: Models for Interpretation*. Edited by Jerome H. Neyrey. Peabody, MA: Hendrickson, 1991.

Saller, Richard. "Slavery and the Roman Family." Pages 65–87 in *Classical Slavery*. Edited by M. I. Finley. London: Frank Cass & Co., 1987.

Shillington, V. George. *2 Corinthians*. Believers Church Bible Commentary. Scottdale, PA: Herald Press, 1998.

Sing the Journey: Hymnal: A Worship Book—Supplement 1. Scottdale, PA: Faith & Life Resources, 2005.

Sing the Story: Hymnal: A Worship Book—Supplement 2. Scottdale, PA: Faith & Life Resources, 2007.

Slavery in Test and Interpretation: Semeia 83/84. Guest edited by Allen Dwight Callahan, Richard A. Horsley, and Abraham Smith. Atlanta, GA: Society of Biblical Literature, 1998.

The United Methodist Hymnal. Nashville, TN: United Methodist Publishing House, 1989.

Wellborn, Lawrence L. "On the Discord in Corinth: 1 Corinthians 1–4 and Ancient Politics." *Journal of Biblical Literature* 106 (1987): 86–107.

Wiedemann, Thomas. *Greek and Roman Slavery*. Baltimore, MD: Johns Hopkins University Press, 1981. Reprinted New York, NY: Routledge, 1988, 1992, 1994.

Wink, Walter. *Engaging the Powers: Discernment and Resistance in a World of Domination.* Minneapolis, MN: Fortress Press, 1992.

Winter, Bruce W. *After Paul Left Corinth: The Influence of Secular Ethics and Social Change.* Grand Rapids, MI: Eerdmans, 2001.

Wire, Antoinette Clark. *The Corinthian Women Prophets: A Reconstruction through Paul's Rhetoric.* Minneapolis, MN: Fortress Press, 1990.

————. "Reclaiming a Theology of Glory from the Corinthian Women Prophets." Pages 36–51 in *Conflict and Community in the Christian Church.* Edited by J. Shannon Clarkson. New York: Women's Division, General Board of Global Ministries of The United Methodist Church, 2000. Reprinted from *Healing for God's World: Remedies from Three Continents.* Kofi Asare Opoku, Kim Yong-Bock, Antoinette Clark Wire. New York: Friendship Press, 1991.

Witherington, Ben, III. *Conflict and Community in Corinth: A Socio-Rhetorical Commentary on 1 and 2 Corinthians.* Grand Rapids, MI: Eerdmans, 1995.

————. *A Week in the Life of Corinth.* Downers Grove, IL: InterVarsity Academic, 2012.

Wren, Brian. "Lord God, Your Love Has Called Us Here." *The United Methodist Hymnal.* Nashville, TN: United Methodist Publishing House, 1989.

Wright, N. Tom. *Paul for Everyone: 1 Corinthians.* London, Louisville, KY: Westminster/JohnKnox Press, 2004.

Zanker, Paul. *The Power of Images in the Age of Augustus.* Trans. Alan Shapiro. Ann Arbor, MI: University of Michigan Press, 1988.

PHOTO AND ILLUSTRATION CREDITS

Page	Credit
17	Reta H. Finger
24	EcoChap / Wikimedia
26	Reta H. Finger
32	Illustration from the 1890 Holman Bible
32	© Blue Guides Limited (Blue Guide Greece, 7th ed.) Used with permission.
33	© Blue Guides Limited (Blue Guide Greece, 7th ed.) Used with permission.
34	Till Niermann / Wikimedia
34	© Blue Guides Limited (Blue Guide Greece, 7th ed.) Used with permission.
36	Wikimedia
36	Aiwok / Wikimedia
37	© Blue Guides Limited (Blue Guide Greece, 7th ed.) Used with permission.
38	I, Grizzli / Wikimedia
39	© Blue Guides Limited (Blue Guide Greece, 7th ed.) Used with permission.
40	Reta H. Finger

41	Anita Rediger
42	© Blue Guides Limited (Blue Guide Greece, 7th ed.) Used with permission.
42	George D. McClain
42	Colmar Painter / Wikimedia
43	Reta H. Finger
44	George D. McClain
44	Euaion Painter / Wikimedia
45	Reta H. Finger
85	Wikimedia
86	Reta H. Finger
87	Reta H. Finger
100	Till Niermann / Wikimedia
107	Reta H. Finger
115	Reta H. Finger
125	Reta H. Finger
126	Anita Rediger
144	Reta H. Finger
156	Reta H. Finger
164	Ted E. Finger
176	Tom Matheny
186	Reta H. Finger
199	Tom Matheny
218	George D. McClain

INDEX

251

THE AUTHORS

In 2009, **Reta Halteman Finger** retired from teaching in the Biblical Studies and Religion department at Messiah College, Grantham, Pennsylvania. Today she occasionally teaches at Eastern Mennonite University in Harrisonburg, Virginia, as affiliate associate professor of New Testament.

The former editor of the Christian feminist magazine, *Daughters of Sarah*, Reta has published three other books, including *Roman House Churches for Today* (1993, 2007), whose format inspired *Creating a Scene in Corinth*. She maintains an active writing ministry through Sunday school columns in the *Mennonite World Review*, *Sojourners* magazine, her Bible study blog at the *Christian Feminism Today* website (www.eewc.com), and other venues.

Reta was born in Harleysville, Pennsylvania. She holds a master's degree from Garrett-Evangelical Seminary and a PhD from Northwestern University, both in Evanston, Illinois. She currently lives in Harrisonburg, Virginia, where she attends Community Mennonite Church. She has two sons, Ted and Brent, and four grandchildren.

George D. McClain was born in Berne, Indiana, of a Mennonite mother and a Methodist father. A graduate of Yale University and Union Theological Seminary,

 he also received a DMin from New York Theological Seminary. Today he is adjunct professor at New York Theological Seminary and The College of New Jersey. He is author of *Claiming All Things for God: Prayer, Discernment, and Ritual for Social Action* (1998) and is one of the coauthors, with his wife, Tilda Norberg, of *The Call: Living Sacramentally—Walking Justly* (2013).

George's interest in social justice ministry was molded by his participation in the Civil Rights Movement, including the 1963 March on Washington and the 1964 Selma-to-Montgomery march. After serving as a United Methodist pastor in Staten Island, he worked for twenty-five years as executive director of the Methodist Federation for Social Action. For fourteen years he was the founder-coordinator of a prison theological education program.

George and Tilda, both United Methodist clergy, have two grown children, Shana and Noah, and two grandchildren. Tilda and George attend the United Methodist Church of St. Paul and St. Andrew in Manhattan, and Olivet Presbyterian Church on Staten Island.